PELICAN BOOKS

A414

THE OLD TESTAMENT PROPHETS

E. W. HEATON

D1096394

E. W. HEATON

THE OLD TESTAMENT PROPHETS

PENGUIN BOOKS

BALTIMORE · MARYLAND

Penguin Books Ltd, Harmondsworth, Middlesex

u.s a.: Penguin Books Inc., 3300 Clipper Mill Road, Baltimore 11, Md

australia: Penguin Books Pty Ltd, 762 Whitehorse Road,
Mitcham, Victoria

—

First published 1958
Reprinted with revisions 1961

—

This book is a completely revised and largely rewritten
edition of *His Servants the Prophets*, published by the S.C.M.
Press in 1949

Copyright © E. W. Heaton, 1958, 1961

—

Made and printed in Great Britain
by R. & R. Clark Ltd
Edinburgh

To the memory of a revered Teacher
S. A. COOK
and to our former colleagues
the Master and Fellows of
Gonville and Caius College
Cambridge

CONTENTS

PREFACE

THIS modest study was first published in 1949 under the title *His Servants the Prophets*, which I have abandoned for the sake of clarity, but not without regret. In preparing this new edition, I have tried to make the book more useful to the general reader, teacher, and student, for whom it was originally written, by incorporating the results of further reading and reflection. In consequence, few pages remain wholly unchanged. The most considerable revision has been made in the third and last chapters. In the former ('The Vocation of the People'), it seemed desirable to state more clearly and emphatically that the Hebrew prophets gave incomparable expression to what was in some measure the common Mosaic faith of Israel. They were far from being traditionalists, but they were certainly heirs to a tradition. In the last chapter ('Faith and Fulfilment'), the importance of kingship in Israelite thought and its bearing on the nature of the prophets' hope have, I trust, been more satisfactorily presented.

Many other sections of the book have been redrafted and expanded and the American Revised Standard Version has been substituted for the English Revised Version in biblical quotations. Considerable attention has been given to the biblical references, which, it is hoped, will be found to reward the effort they are intended to invite. Their purpose is to enable the more industrious reader to gain some familiarity with the actual text of the prophetic books, which, unfortunately, are peculiarly difficult to grasp in consecutive reading. Strings of references may appear tedious, but they are necessary equipment for making any kind of deep penetration into these forbidding Jungle Books. References to literature about the prophets have been excluded from the body of the text, but a guide to further reading is given in an appendix. I have also added another brief appendix, which attempts to display in outline the *prophetic* understanding of Israel's history alongside the political record. A purely political history of Israel (such as is still sometimes taught) leaves out the very factor which is central in the Old Testament – the faith of God's people.

The general plan of the original book, however, remains unaltered and, in a few respects, no attempt has been made to move with the times. The unsuspecting reader should be warned, for example, that in some circles I should be reckoned regrettably old-fashioned for continuing to stress the *distinctive* features of Hebrew prophecy and for remaining unmoved by a number of *formal* features, which its great representatives shared with lesser breeds (both within and without the Law). In this, as in other matters, there is wisdom in the saying that the contents of the bottle matter more than its label and shape. Despite the vigorous search for parallels in the ancient Near East, the historical origins of Hebrew prophecy are still obscure and (what is more important) its essential uniqueness remains unchallenged.

In a most suggestive chapter of his recent book, *Christian Belief and This World*, S.C.M. Press (1956), Dr A. R. Vidler puts to present-day Christians the uncomfortable question, 'Are we also among the prophets?' He comments: 'The fact that the words "prophecy" and "prophet" have not been associated with anything in the living and constant experience of the great churches of christendom or with normal features of the Christian life does not of course mean that there have in reality been no prophecy and prophets in the successive periods of church history. But I do suggest that the neglect not only of the words but of explicit recognition of the gift and endowments which they denote has been a grave source of loss to the church and to the understanding of Christian belief and practice' (p. 76). That loss is manifest when Religion is mistaken for the Reality of God.

St John's College　　　　　　　　　　　　　E. W. HEATON
Oxford

CHAPTER ONE

THE PROPHETIC WRITINGS

THE literature of the Old Testament presents formidable difficulties to the ordinary reader and demands of him a greater effort of historical imagination than any of the other principal parts of the Christian heritage. It is not hard to appreciate why this is so. The books of the Hebrew Bible come from an age and civilization vastly different from ours, and the concern of their authors for the urgent needs of their own day has left its mark in allusions and references with which the modern reader is wholly unfamiliar. The very realism of the Old Testament writers makes their work unreal to us, unless we bridge the gap by patient study.

Life in the circumstances which the twentieth century imposes on most people is too full for them to wish to spend their leisure in the study of an ancient culture simply for its own sake. It would seem, therefore, that the Hebrew Scriptures have had their day and will soon be forgotten, unless our own generation is somehow convinced in an entirely new way that they are worth remembering. Their traditional place in the Christian heritage will not guarantee their preservation at a time when the Christian faith is having to fight to preserve its own distinctive life. If, then, the books of the Old Testament are read and revered in the future, it will be because Christians have re-discovered in them an essential insight into the nature of their profession, which illuminates their vocation as members of the People of God.

OUR APPROACH TO THE OLD TESTAMENT

Those who believe that the Old Testament expounds the inauguration of a unique relationship between God and his world must steadfastly try to understand the Hebrew Scriptures themselves, as and when they were written. If they cannot speak their message when their original meaning is disclosed, their interpreters will never be able to speak it for them. It is useless to devise new methods of interpretation or revive traditional ones, if they succeed merely in retaining the books of the Old Testament in ecclesiastical circulation – in postponing their burial once they are dead. That temptation is seductive at the present time, when so much that is traditional is being challenged and when, therefore, the preservation of the *status quo* seems to be an end good in itself. There are not wanting indications that many would-be champions of the Old Testament have succumbed to the temptation. They tell us that the Hebrew Scriptures must once again be interpreted as the Church has generally understood them – that is to say, allegorically.

The allegorical method of interpreting the Old Testament will be familiar to many English readers from the chapter-headings of the Authorized Version. It is to be seen at its most imaginative in the Song of Solomon, where an anthology of secular love songs is made to speak of Christ and his Church. In essence, the allegorical method of interpretation is little more than a device for combining an ancient authority with a current belief – without appearing to sacrifice either. It was a popular method in the late Greek world of making the outrageous behaviour of the old gods tolerable to a more sensitive civilization. It was the device used by Jewish philosophers, like Philo, in their attempts to commend the Hebrew Scriptures to the cultivated pagan world of their day. It was taken over by some of the New Testament writers to help them expound the Christian gospel to those who had been brought up in the faith of Israel and were steeped in its religious literature. To speak plainly, allegorical interpretation was often a way of making the best of a bad job, a way of making a hallowed tradition or text mean something you wanted it to mean, when its actual meaning was something quite different. The revival in our own day of this method of mishandling the literature of the Old Testament is exceedingly disturbing. It will be obvious how it enables modern religious teachers to present their own particular point of view in a way which suggests that it possesses the authority of Biblical revelation.

Like conjurors, they find in the Old Testament what they themselves have planted there; like ventriloquists, they reduce the prophets to dummies obedient to their own voice. This is not so much interpretation as exploitation; as such, it must be firmly repudiated.

Allegorizing should be carefully distinguished from 'typological interpretation' of which the modern rediscovery is a much more healthy sign. Whereas so-called allegorical interpretation fastens on trivial details of a text and uses them as a flimsy foundation for an elaborate imaginative superstructure, typological interpretation finds in the Old Testament fundamental *types* of the relationship between God and his world, which are developed and filled out by the events of the New Testament.[1] The Suffering Servant of Isaiah, for example, is a type of Christ and was recognised as such by our Lord himself.[2] Typological interpretation, therefore, does not read extraneous notions into the text, nor obliterate the distinction between the Old and New Testaments. It helps, rather, to elucidate the great theological themes which express the unity of God's self-revelation. This unity is nowhere better stated than in the opening verses of the Epistle to the Hebrews: 'In many and various ways God spoke of old to our fathers by the prophets; but in these last days he has spoken to us by a Son.'

We must be grateful, nevertheless, that the early Church kept the Old Testament in allegorical cold-storage at a time when the significance of its original meaning had been forgotten. But now the situation has radically changed. Previously, the problem (even if it was not always fully appreciated) was that of using a body of literature which was too authoritative to be ignored. Now the problem is that of retaining a body of literature which can no longer be regarded as divinely infallible or equally inspired in all its parts, but which has within it a revelation of eternal validity.

Anybody who has not only read the Hebrew Scriptures but also given his mind to them will hesitate to affirm with slick

1. See Romans 5. 14, where Adam is described as 'a type of the one who was to come'.

2. See pp. 87ff., 169.

dogmatic confidence that the Christian must continue to use them because they are the inspired Word of God. In speaking his Word, God neither contradicts himself nor displays the pride and prejudice of ordinary human nature, and of these things the Old Testament writings cannot possibly be acquitted. Popular religion may be able to ignore these facts (for facts they are and not the opinions of a few wicked Higher Critics), but it does so at its peril. What is certain is that true religion cannot be blind to them.

Nor can we be content to say without qualification that Christians should read the Old Testament because it is fulfilled in the New Testament. The Hebrew Scriptures have come from many different levels of spiritual awareness and the New Testament does not and cannot fulfil irreconcilable moral injunctions, nor confirm in any simple way divergent religious traditions. The New Testament is certainly the fulfilment of the central prophetic revelation of the Old Testament, but with equal certainty we may say that it repudiates much of what the Israelites actually believed and said. 'You have heard that it was said to the men of old … *But I say to you*;'[1] Christian fulfilment is founded on Christian discrimination. When the Church took over the Hebrew Canon, it did not relieve Christians of the burden of discrimination (the very idea would have flabbergasted St Paul); it marked out, rather, the sphere in which discrimination should be exercised.

For such discrimination within the Old Testament writings, the true yard-stick (or 'canon') is the Word of God in the New Testament – the Word made flesh, as we meet him in the gospels and find his Person and Work interpreted by the early Church. Essentially, then, we read the Old Testament to discover the beginning of that divine revelation of which the Person and Work of Christ were the climax and fulfilment. Incidentally, without such knowledge, the New Testament itself hangs unintelligible in the air, having (like Melchizedek) neither beginning of days nor end of life.

The Person of Christ has, of course, been represented as the fulfilment and elucidation of many other traditions – of

1. Matthew 5. 21–2, 27–8, 31–2, 33–4, 38–9, 43–4.

philosophical thought, for example, and of 'higher' religions other than Judaism. The appreciation of the relationship between Christ, who is fully the Way, the Truth, and the Life, and other noble ways, truths, and lives is a vital part of the theologian's task, and the Bible itself (which, it should never be forgotten, begins with the Creation narrative) does not so much forbid this wider theological exploration as emphatically demand it. To repudiate philosophy and the comparative study of religion is not truly biblical, but narrowly biblicist. Nevertheless, the Old Testament is in a special position. It is not simply one among many 'preparations for the gospel', because it records the immediate context in which Christ came and that context was not only one of religious thought, but also (and primarily) that of a particular historical community. The unique importance of the Old Testament depends not so much on the intrinsic value of its religious 'ideas,' as on the Christian belief that God, the Ultimate Reality, deliberately chose to reveal himself to the world through the life of a particular historical community – the life of Israel and the Christian Church.

The early Church took over the Old Testament Canon of Scripture, because it bore witness to the continuous life of a people in which the God and Father of our Lord Jesus Christ had manifestly disclosed his nature and purpose. God had revealed himself, not in a number of books (nor in books of numbers!), but in making and remaking, calling and recalling his people Israel. The Old Testament writings record the manifold life of that people, its chequered history, its religious response and apostasy, its laws, priestly systems, prophecy, politics, songs, and sagas. It is often difficult to see the wood for the trees, but when the literature as a whole is related to the life of Israel, the nature of God is manifestly (though not uniformly) revealed.

In studying any part of the Old Testament, the Christian is involved, therefore, in a pursuit which is at least four-fold: (1) the discovery of what the particular passage means in its original language and situation; (2) the discovery of the light which is shed by that meaning on the nature and purpose of God in and through Israel; (3) the discovery of the relationship between the revelation of God in Israel and the revelation of God in Christ; (4) the response to that revelation within the community of the New Israel – the Christian Church. In a word, we read and study the Old Testament to find God addressing us through the Old Israel, so that we may respond to him the more readily in the life and witness of the New Israel. The revealing and redemptive history which begins in the Hebrew Scriptures is still being made.

The spokesmen and interpreters of God's purpose in calling Israel to be his people were, as we shall see, pre-eminently the prophets. It is nothing less than tragic that their witness has for centuries been virtually ignored in the life and thinking of the Church and it is nothing less than essential that the Church should rediscover its prophetic vocation.

The following chapters are intended to stimulate thought and study with this immense and vital task in view. Our plan is to explore Old Testament prophecy along four main lines. First, we shall consider the uniqueness of the prophetic consciousness, since it was from this that the prophets' compelling conviction and profound insight sprang. Second, we shall try to show how the prophets understood the uniqueness of Israel's vocation as the People of God, how that understanding led to conflict with their contemporaries, and how amid this conflict they made their tremendous affirmations of faith. Third, we shall try to see how the prophets welded their nomadic moral tradition with their own incomparable awareness of communion with the living God. Finally, we shall be observing how, during and after the period of the Exile, the prophets proclaimed the kingly Rule of God and the firm conviction that one day it would be known throughout the world. This hope was never actually realized in the experience of the Jewish community. But it was realized, completely and finally, in the life, death, and resurrection of Jesus, whose prophetic ministry was itself a proclamation that the Kingdom of God had come. Such is our plan.

Before, however, we begin our exploration of the prophetic writings along these four paths, we should do well to recognize what a bewildering jungle we shall be trying to penetrate. We must, therefore, first attempt a rapid survey of the prophetic books, pointing out as we proceed some of the more obvious pitfalls, and equipping ourselves with that minimum of historical and literary data which our task demands.

THE PROPHETIC BOOKS

We may begin our survey of the prophetic writings with a copy of the Revised Version (or, better still, the Revised Standard Version) of the Old Testament in front of us, its pages open at the place where Isaiah begins. At our right hand, we find three large books (Isaiah, Jeremiah, and Ezekiel), two small books (Lamentations and Daniel), and twelve tracts of unequal length, each with a name at its head.

Daniel and Lamentations may be dismissed from our consideration immediately, since in the Hebrew Bible both these works are placed – not with the prophets – but in that miscellaneous group of Old Testament books called 'The Writings'.[1] This is obviously where Lamentations properly belongs, since it is made up of five dirge-like psalms, describing with a wealth of graphic detail the fall of Jerusalem in 586 B.C. The ascription of the work to Jeremiah in the title lacks good authority and it is probable that the psalms have come from the pen of more than one anonymous author.

The book of Daniel is equally out of place among the prophets. Its popular stories and highly symbolic visions were written in loyal scribal circles (related in many ways to the sect brought to light by the recent discovery of the Dead Sea Scrolls), when the very existence of the Jewish community was threatened by the persecuting Greek king, Antiochus Epiphanes, during the years 167–164 B.C. It is a document of immense spiritual courage and great theological interest, but only confusion has resulted from its being read as the prophetic book *par excellence*. The device adopted by its author of addressing his contemporaries through the medium of an

1. The Writings include: Psalms, Proverbs, Job, Song of Songs, Ruth, Lamentations, Ecclesiastes, Esther, Daniel, Ezra, Nehemiah, and Chronicles.

ancient sage has encouraged the erroneous notion that prediction rather than proclamation was the primary business of the prophet.[1]

In this rapid survey, we shall be concerned, therefore, only with the three large books (Isaiah, Jeremiah, and Ezekiel) and the twelve small tracts. The name given to the latter collection – the 'Minor Prophets' – is appropriate only to their size, for with the three books of the other group – the 'Major Prophets' – they represent the literary record of one of the most remarkable phenomena known to the historians of religion.

The Minor Prophets

We may start our exploration with HOSEA, one of the twelve minor prophets, and then work forward. The inscription to this book suggests that the prophet began his ministry just after the middle of the eighth century (about 745 B.C.), when the prosperous northern kingdom of Israel, the land of his birth, was heading towards her destruction at the hands of Assyria in 721 B.C. It is obvious that the fourteen chapters before us have been written down by somebody other than Hosea, since the first of them is biographical. The combination of biographical and autobiographical material in one and the same book is a fairly clear indication that the work has passed through the hands of an editor drawing on a number of different sources.[2] It is also worth noticing that the translators have been forced to include many variant readings in the notes at the foot of each page – a sure indication that the Hebrew text has come down to us in a rather bad state of preservation.

We know nothing of JOEL, whose name heads the next book, except that he was the son of Pethuel (and that is not very helpful). The evidence supplied by the work itself, however, makes it plausible to ascribe it to a prophet *writing* about 400 B.C. This dating is confirmed by the author's extensive

---

1. See pp. 124–30.
2. The chief later additions in Hosea are: 1. 7; 1. 10–2. 1; 2. 21–3; 3. 5; and (probably) 14. 1–9.

borrowings from his predecessors [1] – a feature which characterizes the literary and more stylized prophecy of the period following the exile of the Jews in Babylon in the sixth century (586–520 B.C.)

We come now to the very important book of AMOS. Again, we know nothing of his parents, his family, or his friends; nothing of his connexions with the prophets who came before him. The sparse biographical notes in the book (1. 1; 7. 14) tell us that he was a sheep-farmer from the east of Judah and that he did a seasonal job as a 'pricker' of sycamore-trees (the fruit of which was punctured to hasten ripening). His social status is peculiarly difficult to determine, but so articulate a critic of the corruption of urban society can hardly have been a mere country bumpkin. He may well have been a small, independent farmer.

Scholars argue about the exact date of Amos' ministry. It certainly came within the reign of Jeroboam II (787–747 B.C.), but within this period some favour an early date (about 760 B.C.) and some a later one, when it was beginning to be obvious that Assyria would soon be in the field again threatening Israel's independence. We shall not be far wrong if we think of Amos as leaving his sheep and sycamores about 750 B.C. to denounce in the northern kingdom of Israel what Sir John Falstaff (as he reviewed his ragged recruits) called 'the cankers of a calm world and a long peace'. For about half a century, Israel had been unmolested by the great powers, and the resulting period of peace and prosperity had given the unscrupulous speculators and get-rich-quicks their golden opportunity. Israel's decay, so far from being held in check by religious principles, was being hastened by the superstitious and futile cult which flourished at the local sanctuaries. The state of the country was ruinous, but it needed a prophet of the courage and calibre of Amos to make the people realize that they were not only in danger but doomed to destruction. God had rejected them and was about to give effect to his judgement.

1. In the following passages it is Joel who appears to be the borrower: 1. 15 (Isa. 13. 6); 2. 2 (Zeph. 1. 15); 2. 3 (Isa. 51. 3; Ezek. 36. 35); 2.10 (Isa. 13. 10); 2. 32 (Obad. 17); 3. 10 (Isa. 2. 4; Mic. 4. 3); 3. 16 (Amos 1. 2; Isa. 13. 13); 3. 17 (Ezek. 36. 11; Isa. 52. 1).

It is very remarkable that we have any record at all of the sermons of a man who did his preaching over 2,500 years ago. How the discourses of Amos came to be preserved is a matter for scholarly speculation. We do not know for certain that Amos had either disciples or secretary, but the preservation of his message proves beyond dispute that he was not an isolated voice crying in the wilderness. How much (if anything) the prophet himself set down in writing, or revised, so to speak, before publication, we have no means of discovering. Here and there, a touch of irony strongly suggests that we are in close touch with the original author and it is clear that one master spirit has left its stamp on the bulk of the book. It is equally clear, however, that we owe some small parts of it to the enlightened men of the succeeding centuries, who preserved the teaching of all the great prophets.[1]

Despite the literary process through which the book has passed, it still bears the marks of its origin in the spoken word. The short paragraphs (or 'oracles') of which it is composed are clearly related to the prophet's style of preaching, although the order of these oracles as they are now arranged is almost certainly the work, not of Amos, but of his editors. They have sometimes been grouped according to their subject matter, but, more often, they have been strung together without much thought of logical or chronological order. This explains why the prophetic books are so disconnected and difficult to read and why many of them contain passages from an altogether different source. A carefree attitude to authorship and literary integrity was, of course, universal in the ancient world and it finds further illustration in the little post-exilic fragment of OBADIAH – the shortest and perhaps the least illuminating book in the Old Testament. It is mainly a denunciation of Edom, concocted (as the marginal references of the Revised Standard Version indicate) from other prophetic writings.[2]

The book of JONAH, which follows, is usually dated about 350 B.C. It is unique among the prophetic books in that it is a

1. Amos 1. 1; 1. 9–12; 2. 4–5; 4. 13; 5. 8–9; 9. 5–6; 9. 11–15.
2. Isa. 34; 63. 1–6; Jer. 49. 7–22; Ezek. 25. 12–14; 35; Amos 1. 11–12; Mal. 1. 2–5.

work of didactic fiction – a kind of extended parable – written round the name of one of the ancient prophets (mentioned in II Kings 14. 25). The great fish (it is not called a whale) was just the sort of fantastic wonder in which the Eastern story-teller delighted and here it is used to sauce the moral that God was no less interested in the Gentile nations than in his Chosen People. Israel had been set free from the Babylonian Exile in which she had been swallowed up and yet she was not making use of her opportunities to be a light to lighten the Gentiles.[1] The final editor of the book, considering that a psalm would further enhance the tale, interpolated what is now the second chapter.

MICAH, a peasant farmer of Moresheth in Judah, whose name heads the next collection of oracles, was responsible for the material now contained in the first three chapters of the book. As a contemporary of Isaiah, Micah denounced both the northern and southern kingdoms during the last quarter of the eighth century B.C. The remainder of the book is a mixed compendium of oracles, which for the most part express the hope of men living in exile that they would be restored to their own land, there to enjoy the blessings of the Reign of God.[2] Once again, we are reminded how it is only our failure to appreciate Hebrew literary methods which has given currency to the absurd notion that it is more pious to ascribe all the contents of a book to the 'title-prophet' than to welcome the aid of scholarly analysis. The complaint we may justly make against some of the earlier biblical scholars is not that they 'carved up' the books of the Bible, but that they were wedded to the strange idea that a piece of literature is intrinsically more valuable if we can name its author. The result was that they often overlooked the profound import-ance of anonymous prophecy. Their presuppositions are well illustrated, for example, by the many attempts to prove that Mic. 6. 1–8 is a genuine fragment of the prophet's preaching. The passage, of course, stands in its own right, whatever its origin, as a perfect summary of prophetic faith, requiring no further authentication.

1. Jer. 51. 34, 44; cf. Ps. 74. 13–14; Isa. 51. 9.
2. Note that Mic. 4. 1–3 occurs also in Isa. 2. 2-4.

The book NAHUM, which follows as we turn the pages, has very little spiritual significance. It combines fragments of an acrostic poem (1. 2–9) with a magnificent but terrible ode, celebrating the imminent collapse of Nineveh, the capital of Assyria, in 612 B.C. A modern translation will help us recapture something of the prophet's grim realism, as he gleefully looks forward to the dismembering of Israel's tyrannical oppressor. Despite the conventional prophetic formula in 2. 13 and 3. 5, it must be admitted that this book is far removed from the main prophetic tradition and those who seek its origin and purpose in some liturgical context may well be working on the right lines.

A cultic background has also been suggested for the book of HABAKKUK, of which the first two chapters deal with the rise of the Chaldeans and the problem raised by the suffering of the righteous at the hands of the wicked. It may be dated tentatively about 600 B.C., except for the psalm of the third chapter, which must be ascribed to an author of the post-exilic age. The earliest known commentary on this book, probably written in the second half of the first century B.C., was one of the Dead Sea Scrolls discovered in 1947–8. It may be no mere accident that it deals only with the first two chapters and shows no knowledge of the psalm. But whenever the psalm was added, its splendid conclusion – so apposite to a harvest-thanksgiving service after a disappointing season – is always worth recalling:

> Though the fig tree do not blossom,
> nor fruit be on the vines,
> the produce of the olive fail
> and the fields yield no food,
> the flock be cut off from the fold
> and there be no herd in the stalls,
> yet I will rejoice in the LORD,
> I will joy in the God of my salvation.[1]

1. Hab. 3. 17–18. A comment is necessary on the use of the word LORD. The Revised Standard Version, like the English Revised Version, follows the Authorized (King James) Version in avoiding both the term 'Jehovah' and the term 'Yahweh' for the Divine Name, which is translated LORD (or in certain cases GOD) printed in capitals. In the Preface to the Revised Standard Version, the following statement is made: 'While it is

This is how Hebrew faith at its best answered intellectual difficulties at their worst.

The central passage of the next book, ZEPHANIAH, is familiar to many people from the famous Latin hymn, *Dies Irae*, which it inspired (1. 7–16). The spirit of Amos breathes again in this prophet's ruthless denunciation of idolatrous worship, in his forthright attack on the ruling classes of Judah, and in his fearless expectation that a great day of divine reckoning – the Day of the Lord – was imminent.[1] The historical background of the work is again difficult to determine. Some scholars relate Zephaniah's oracles to an invasion of the Mediterranean area by bands of Scythian marauders, which, it is supposed, took place about 626 B.C.

The five reported declarations of HAGGAI, which follow, are different from anything we have encountered so far.[2] Not only are they addressed primarily to individuals (the governor Zerubbabel and the high-priest Joshua), but also their main purpose is to promote the rebuilding of the Temple in 520 B.C. This restoration is one of the main interests of the next and greater prophet ZECHARIAH, whose own work con-

---

almost if not quite certain that the Name was originally pronounced "Yahweh", this pronunciation was not indicated when the Masoretes added vowel signs to the consonantal Hebrew text. To the four consonants YHWH of the Name, which had come to be regarded as too sacred to be pronounced, they attached vowel signs indicating that in its place should be read the Hebrew word *Adonai* meaning "Lord" (or *Elohim* meaning "God"). ... The form "Jehovah" is of late medieval origin; it is a combination of the consonants of the Divine Name and the vowels attached to it by the Masoretes but belonging to an entirely different word. The sound of Y is represented by J and the sound of W by V, as in Latin. For two reasons the Committee has returned to the more familiar usage of the King James Version: (1) the word "Jehovah" does not accurately represent any form of the Name ever used in Hebrew; and (2) the use of any proper name for the one and only God, as though there were other gods from whom He had to be distinguished, was discontinued in Judaism before the Christian era and is entirely inappropriate for the universal faith of the Christian Church.' While the usage of the Revised Standard Version is followed exactly in all quotations taken from it, the form 'God' (with only an initial capital) has been used otherwise.

1. The book contains a number of editorial insertions: Zeph. 2. 3, 7, 8–12; 3. 8–20.

2. (*a*) Hag. 1. 1–15; (*b*) 2. 1–9; (*c*) 2. 10–14; (*d*) 2. 15–19; (*e*) 2. 20–3

sists of eight visions,[1] with introductory (1. 1–6) and conclud-
ing oracles (6. 9–8. 23) – all contained in the first eight chapters of the book. Between 520 and 518 B.C., that is, about
seventy years after the destruction of Jerusalem by the Babylonians, Zechariah affirms his conviction that God will restore
its Temple and establish Zerubbabel and Joshua, as king and
high-priest respectively.[2] The moral conditions of this restoration which Zechariah announces are strongly reminiscent of
the teaching of his predecessors, called now, we may notice,
'the former prophets'.[3] It is generally agreed that the last six
chapters of the book (9–14) are not the work of Zechariah,
although scholarly opinion has not crystallized to a more
precise dating for them than the third century B.C. Even this
is more an informed guess than a calculation made on the
basis of clear evidence. Although anonymous and difficult to
interpret, these oracles of catastrophe and hope bear witness
to a confidence in God's ultimate victory in the world with a
vigour seldom surpassed in the Old Testament.

The last of the twelve minor prophets confirms our asser-
tion that the names at the head of the various books are sometimes little more than an editorial convenience and by no
means always describe the author of the succeeding oracles.
MALACHI is simply the Hebrew for 'my messenger'.[4] These
anonymous oracles were delivered about 460 B.C. It will be
noticed that the prophet has largely abandoned the former
method of direct proclamation and now tries to argue the
point in a question-and-answer presentation of his message.
We get the impression that he was a faithful and modest
pastor, faced with despondency in his flock and with the
degeneration which despondency breeds – slovenly worship,
corrupt legal practice, divorce, social injustice, and cynicism.
His good qualities and his weaknesses are those which are
characteristic of prophecy in its declining years after about
520 B.C.

1. (a) Zech. 1. 7–17; (b) 1. 18–21; (c) 2. 1–5; (d) 3. 1–10; (e) 4. 1–6, 10–
14; (f) 5. 1–4; (g) 5. 5–11; (h) 6. 1–8.
2. Joshua's name seems to have replaced that of Zerubbabel in Zech.
6. 11.
3. Zech. 1. 4–6; 5. 1–11; 7. 4–14.
4. Mal. 3. 1; cf. Hag. 1. 13.

The Major Prophets

We come now to the second phase of our rapid exploration of the prophetic writings and glance at the Major Prophets – the books of Isaiah, Jeremiah, and Ezekiel. When no two scholars are agreed about many of the hundred-and-one literary problems which they (inevitably) raise, it will be obvious that we cannot hope to do more than eliminate some of the difficulties which stand in the way of ordinary intelligent reading.

The book of ISAIAH is a vast and very untidy anthology containing: (*a*) oracles from Isaiah, the son of Amoz, whose prophetic ministry in Jerusalem lasted from about 742 B.C. to the end of the century; (*b*) oracles from an anonymous prophet (usually called Second- or Deutero-Isaiah), who was a member of the Jewish community living in Babylon about 540 B.C.; and (*c*) a large number of important miscellaneous passages of which the oracles contained in Chapters 56–66 form a fairly unified group, reflecting conditions in Palestine some time after the rebuilding of the Temple in 516 B.C.

The material which represents the preaching of Isaiah of Jerusalem is roughly that which remains in Chapters 1–39, when we have identified as insertions made by later editors such passages as the extract from II Kings 18. 13–20. 19 in Chapters 36–9, the poems of final judgement and deliverance in Chapters 24–7 and 34–5, some of the oracles of doom against foreign nations in Chapters 13–23,[1] and various sections which clearly reflect the outlook of the period following the fall of Jerusalem in 586 B.C.[2] It would be wholly mistaken to suppose that these passages from writers later than Isaiah are being or can be dismissed as unimportant glosses. They are no less significant than (say) the eighteenth-century additions which we may detect in an Elizabethan house. They have their meaning both as part of the final composition and as witnesses to the outlook of their own period. It is important,

1. Isa. 13. 1–22 (Babylon); 14. 1–23 (Babylon); 15. 1–16. 14 (Moab); 21. 1–10 (Babylon); 21. 11–12 (Edom); 21. 13–17 (Kedar); 23. 1–14 (Tyre and Sidon).
2. Isa. 1. 27–31; 2. 2–5; 4. 2–6; 11. 10–16; 12. 1–6; 19. 16–25; 23. 15–18; 29. 17–24; 30. 18–26; 32. 1–8; 32. 15–20; 33. 1–24.

nevertheless, that we should identify the oracles which may with safety be attributed to the prophet Isaiah himself. Probably, we shall not be far from the facts if we take it that he made two written collections of his prophecies; the first early in his ministry, when his message was rejected by the Judean king, Ahaz,[1] and the second towards the end of his ministry, when Judah failed to heed his warnings about the consequences of intriguing with Egypt.[2] Both of these collections appear to have been spliced with oracles from a later period of the prophet's ministry, among which it is relatively easy to identify those on the subject of the threat from Assyria, which nearly overwhelmed Jerusalem in 701 B.C.[3]

If we are daunted by these literary complexities, we may take heart from the knowledge that the text of this untidy book has been transmitted with amazing fidelity through the centuries. Only a few years ago, the most ancient witness to the Hebrew text of Isaiah was no earlier than the tenth century A.D. In 1947–8, however, the sensational discovery among the Dead Sea Scrolls of a beautifully preserved scroll containing the whole of the book (Chapters 1–66) pushed back our evidence of its text over a thousand years – perhaps to the second century B.C. It is astonishing and reassuring to learn that the traditional medieval manuscripts, upon which our translations have hitherto relied, have preserved a text agreeing to a remarkable degree with that of the Dead Sea scroll. Thus we have been brought nearer than the greatest optimist ever dared hope to the time when the prophet's disciples and editors first completed their book.

The superb series of poems which make up Chapters 40–55 of the book of Isaiah was written by an anonymous prophet who lived among his countrymen exiled in Babylon a century and a half after the death of Isaiah of Jerusalem. Cyrus, the king of Persia, who conquered Babylon in 539 B.C. and allowed the Jewish exiles to return home, is twice mentioned explicitly in the book (44. 28; 45. 1). The prophet wrote just before the

1. Most of the oracles in Chapters 1–8.
2. Most of the oracles in Chapters 28–31.
3. Isa. 10. 5–16; 10. 24–7; 10. 28–32; 14. 24–7; 22. 1–14; 29. 1–8; 30. 27–33; 31. 4–9.

change of régime. We know nothing about him, except that he was a man of literary genius and unprecedented theological insight, who matched the hour of the Jews' greatest need, when they were in danger of forsaking the faith of their fathers. He met the dejection of the exiled Judeans with undaunted conviction and urged that the despair of the present time was only the prelude to the New Age which God was about to inaugurate. The imminence of the Coming of the Lord is the theme of the fourteen poems which make up the first half of the book (Chapters 40–48)[1] and Israel's redemption is the theme of the seven poems of the second half (Chapters 49–55).[2] As the two series of poems are continuous and singularly free from surface difficulties and many of the knotty historical problems which other prophetic books present, we can – with pleasure and immense profit – read the whole work at a single sitting. To appreciate the tremendous range of the prophet's vision is the first step towards understanding his message; and the lyrical and dramatic style of which he was so great a master grips the reader with a peculiar intensity.

The last eleven chapters of Isaiah (56–66), sometimes called 'Trito-Isaiah', reflect a haunting sense of the uncertainty of life in Jerusalem after some of the Jews had started to trickle home from exile. One finds on reading them a curious blend of visionary faith and practical interest in the new Temple and its worship. It is extremely probable that this group of oracles – diverse in theme and uneven in quality – has come from some of the disciples of Second Isaiah, who tried to bring to bear their master's insight[3] on the difficult problems of an age of restoration and reconstruction.

JEREMIAH, to whose book we now turn, had a secretary –

---

1. The fourteen poems (following J. Muilenburg's analysis in *The Interpreter's Bible*) are as follows: (a) Isa. 40. 1–11; (b) 40. 12–31; (c) 41. 1–42. 4; (d) 42. 5–17; (e) 42. 18–43. 7; (f) 43. 8–13; (g) 43. 14–44. 5; (h) 44. 6–8, 21–3; (i) 44. 9–20; (j) 44. 24–45. 13; (k) 45. 14–25; (l) 46. 1–13; (m) 47. 1–15; (n) 48. 1–22.

2. The seven poems of the second half are as follows: (a) Isa. 49. 1–26; (b) 50. 1–11; (c) 51. 1–16; (d) 51. 17–52. 12; (e) 52. 13–53. 12; (f) 54. 1–17; (g) 55. 1–13.

3. See especially Isa. 57. 14–21.

Baruch – and he made all the difference. The work moves in a superficially orderly fashion from oracles (Chapters 1–25) to stories of the prophet's ministry (Chapters 26–45), followed by a compendium of passages (not by Jeremiah) on foreign nations (Chapters 46–51). The book ends with a historical appendix (Chapter 52) taken by an editor from II Kings (24. 18–25. 21, 27–30). The main body of the work (Chapters 1–45) has been fairly thoroughly edited. This means that, while relatively few passages have to be wholly discounted when we try to reconstruct Jeremiah's own preaching,[1] we find that a great part of the material has been 'touched up' and idealized – probably by Baruch and his colleagues. We can, therefore, always be fairly sure of the prophet's general meaning, but there is often room for more than one opinion when we come to finer details. Jeremiah witnessed the final collapse of Judah as an independent kingdom and went into exile in Egypt a broken man and an apparent failure. It is, however, to his forty years' ministry (626–586 B.C.) that we turn for the clearest evidence of the permanent significance of pre-exilic prophecy. His life and work provide one of the best explanations of the claim of Jesus that he had come to 'fill out' the revelation which God gave to his ancient people.

EZEKIEL, the last of the books of the Major Prophets, is the despair of both Old Testament scholars and the ordinary reader. We have to choose between making a frank admission that these forty-eight chapters represent a compilation of which the proper analysis has so far escaped us, and accepting as sole author a prophet to whom we must attribute an almost inconceivable diversity of outlook. The physical and spiritual gymnastics with which the second choice credits Ezekiel obviate our literary problems only by raising much more difficult questions of their own. As the book now stands, it includes: (*a*) oracles apparently delivered in Jerusalem before the fall of the city in 586 B.C. (Chapters 1–24); (*b*) oracles against foreign nations (Chapters 25–32); (*c*) oracles apparently delivered in Babylon describing the coming restora-

1. Jer. 3. 15–18; 10. 1–16; 16. 14–21; 17. 5–13; 17. 19–27; 23. 34–40; 25. 8–14; 25. 15–29; 30–1 (except 31. 2–6, 15–22, 31–4); 32. 16–41; 33 1–26; 40. 7–41. 18.

tion of the exiles to Jerusalem (Chapters 33–9); and (d) an idealized vision of the restored Jerusalem, with a detailed 'blue-print' of the new Temple, its plan, priesthood, and worship (Chapters 40–8).

It is obvious that the book of Ezekiel has been compiled according to a pattern similar to that which we find in the books of Isaiah and Jeremiah. First, a collection of oracles delivered in Jerusalem; second, a section on foreign nations; third, a collection of oracles delivered in Babylon on the theme of restoration; and, finally, a section dealing more concretely with the detailed problems of reconstruction in Jerusalem. Although a compiler has obviously been at work on Ezekiel, there is wide disagreement about the extent of his contribution. If he is responsible for the strong stamp of a single mind on the whole book, he edited his material more thoroughly than (say) the editor of the book of Isaiah. It is impossible to deny (but equally difficult to accept) the view that the single mind was that of the prophet Ezekiel himself.

On the face of it, Ezekiel's call to the prophetic ministry came to him in Babylon in 593 B.C. among the exiles of the first deportation of 597 B.C. and he never returned to Palestine. The fact that many of his prophecies are addressed to the people of Jerusalem has led some scholars to the view that the work of a contemporary of Jeremiah has been arbitrarily transferred by an editor from Jerusalem to Babylon, and other scholars to the compromise of postulating for the prophet a double ministry – first in Jerusalem and afterwards in Babylon. Nobody with any respect for the discipline of historical reconstruction will wish to dogmatize in the present chaotic state of scholarly discussion. Although the personality and the characteristic teaching of the prophet must remain uncertain, it may fairly be assumed that the bulk of the material now ascribed to him gives us genuine prophetic insight into the critical religious situation of Israel in the sixth century B.C.

We are now in a position to review this succession of prophets, bearing in mind that no one figure may be said to have embodied – or even to have influenced – the *whole* religious life of his age. In the *pre-exilic period*, we have: in the eighth century: Amos, Hosea, Micah, and Isaiah; and in the seventh century: Zephaniah, Nahum, Habakkuk, and Jeremiah. The imperial background of the former group is dominated by Assyria and of the latter by Babylon.

Thoughts of restoration and reconstruction were uppermost in the prophecy of the *exilic period*: Second Isaiah, Ezekiel, Isaiah 56–66, Haggai, and Zechariah. *After 500 B.C.,* Obadiah, Malachi, Joel, and Jonah show the prophetic flame still alight but flickering before its final extinction. There is, in addition, a vast quantity of anonymous oracles from different periods after the fall of Jerusalem, now interpolated in the various books.

Such a survey as this should call into question and cause us to modify any view of prophetic revelation which finds its authority exclusively either in the religious experience of the few great individual prophets whose names we know, or in the exact form of their words as they have been reported and transmitted to us. The latter dependence is sometimes unsafe and the former always too narrow. The very existence of a great bulk of anonymous prophetic oracles and the enormous labours which have been devoted to these writings by editors during a period of up to five hundred years disclose horizons far wider than those we are accustomed to think of as defining the 'prophetic period'. The difficulties we encounter in reading these books and in trying to establish the original preaching of the individual prophets are often difficulties caused by their very popularity in the long period during which they continued to influence the religious life of Israel. When their meaning is hard to decipher, it is often because, like the pages of an old and treasured prayer-book, the text has been 'thumbed' and annotated through centuries of use and meditation. In a rather similar way, the teaching of the prophets has been annotated in the life of the Christian Church and it is now sometimes difficult to discover its original force. It is quite clear that the modified forms which the faith of the prophets has assumed in later Jewish and Christian tradition are in their own way revealing. There are, however, times when the original inspiration has become so clouded over that a direct return to it is necessary. Our own age is one of those periods. Even those who are most sensitive to the value of tradition must suspect that nothing less than a direct return to the great prophets themselves is demanded by our present condition. We need their force and simplicity to blast us out of the bog of complexities and theological half-truths in which we are floundering.

This is the point at which to admit that we do not know exactly how the teaching of the prophets passed into the religious tradition of post-exilic Judaism. There is no certain evidence even about the process through which their oracles passed from the spoken to the written word. Jeremiah is the only prophet who is reported to have had a secretary and the account of his activities in Jer. 36 sheds more light on the problem than any other single Old Testament passage. The prophet is said to have been commanded by God to take a roll and record all the oracles he had delivered during his ministry of twenty years (verse 2). The purpose of the collection was to provoke the people to repentance at a critical juncture of Judah's history (605 B.C.), when the threat from Babylon began to loom large (verse 3). Jeremiah called for the services of Baruch, the scribe, to whom he dictated the prophecies. This is the first explicit reference in the Old Testament to the writing of a *collection* of prophetic oracles, but, we must notice, it provides no proof either that Jeremiah himself could not write, or that he had not recorded any of his oracles on previous occasions. Nor does it necessarily mean that the prophet was changing his method and abandoning direct personal preaching for the written message. This was a special occasion. It was desperately urgent that the people should be warned of the coming disaster and Jeremiah himself was debarred (for some reason unrevealed) from going to the Temple (verse 5). The roll which was dictated personally by the prophet represented, therefore, the credentials of Baruch (verses 17–18). As the story is unfolded with great dramatic artistry, we learn how the message was read three times on that fast day in December – to the people (verse 10), to the senior statesmen of Judah (verse 15), and, finally, to the king himself (verse 21). Unlike Josiah, his father (see II Kings 22. 11), the king showed no signs of penitence on hearing the word of the Lord (verse 24), but contemptuously slashed the roll with a pen-knife as it was being read and, bit by bit, threw it into the fire (verse 23). The narrator is at pains to emphasize that God's Word is not thus lightly disposed of and that, therefore, another roll was written (verses 27–32). It is difficult to generalize with confidence about the composition of the prophetic books on the basis of this single account. It is possible, but by no means certain, that Baruch's second roll was the nucleus of the book of Jeremiah as we now have it. It is probable, but again by no means certain, that other prophets were well served by disciples and scribes. Isaiah's much-quoted declaration, 'Bind up the testimony, seal the teaching among my disciples,'[1] clearly refers to written prophecy, but it has been plausibly suggested that the prophet was speaking of sealing his teaching not *among* his *disciples*, but *from* the eyes of the *learned*. Although the recent emphasis on the importance of the oral transmission of prophecy is valuable and illuminating, there is much to be said for the less extreme view that oral tradition and written records existed side by side in pre-exilic Israel.

It is, perhaps, not without significance that Jeremiah's roll was first read 'in the chamber of Gemariah the son of Shaphan the secretary' and that Gemariah was among the high administrative officials who 'urged the king not to burn the scroll'.[2] It was also in a scribe's chamber that these friendly officials deposited the roll before they went to see the king.[3] Such evidence may well indicate that Baruch's contribution to the preservation of Jeremiah's oracles was no isolated example and that the scribes, who made up the educated section of the community, were responsible for editing the prophetic literature of Israel during and after the crisis of the Exile. That the idea of written collections of prophecies was familiar in the sixth century B.C. is attested by references to the roll which was handed to Ezekiel (to eat!) as a sign of his prophetic commission and to the enormous flying roll in one of the visions of Zechariah, which, it was said, would judge the iniquity of the land.[4]

1. Isa. 8. 16; cf. 30. 8.   2. Jer. 36. 10, 25.
3. Jer. 36. 20.   4. Ezek. 2. 9–3. 3; Zech. 5. 1–4.

Whatever the history of their compilation, we do know that the four great prophetic anthologies of Isaiah, Jeremiah, Ezekiel, and 'The Twelve' were regarded as authoritative about 180 B.C., when Ben Sira (the author of the book Ecclesiasticus) wrote his roll-call of the heroes of Israel.[1] They are also mentioned by Ben Sira's grandson in the delightful and instructive preface he composed for his translation of Ecclesiasticus from Hebrew into Greek:

> Ye are intreated therefore to read with favour and attention, and to pardon us, if in any parts of what we have laboured to interpret, we may seem to fail in some of the phrases. For things originally spoken in Hebrew have not the same force in them, when they are translated into another tongue: and not only these, but *the law itself, and the prophecies, and the rest of the books*, have no small difference, when they are spoken in their original language. ... I thought it therefore most necessary for me to apply some diligence and travail to interpret this book; applying indeed much watchfulness and skill in that space of time to bring the book to an end, and set it forth for them also, who in the land of their sojourning are desirous to learn, fashioning their manners beforehand, so as to live according to the law.

This passage from the Apocrypha gives good advice to all who would understand the faith of the prophets. Their oracles were spoken in an unfamiliar idiom and collected in a way which often appears to us quite chaotic. They demand, as Ecclesiasticus demanded of its author's grandson, 'some diligence and travail'. It will be fully rewarded if it serves the practical end which Ben Sira's grandson had in view.

1. Ecclesiasticus 48. 20–5 (Isaiah); 49. 6–7 (Jeremiah); 49. 8–9 (Ezekiel); 49. 10 ('The Twelve').

CHAPTER TWO

THE VOCATION OF THE PROPHETS

You cannot go very far in reading the prophetic writings without coming across a passage like the following:

> Thus says the LORD of hosts: 'Do not listen to the words of the prophets who prophesy to you, filling you with vain hopes; they speak visions of their own minds, not from the mouth of the LORD.'[1]

Such a denunciation of the prophets by a prophet is extremely perplexing, until we appreciate that the terms 'prophet' and 'prophesying' have a very wide range of meaning in the Old Testament and so inevitably cover much which illuminates the vocation of men like Amos, Isaiah, and Jeremiah, not directly but by contrast.

The feature common to all prophets in the ancient world is that they claimed to speak with the authority of their god. They were essentially *spokesmen*. This basic characteristic is well illustrated by two alternative descriptions of the relationship between Moses and Aaron in the book Exodus. In the first, Aaron is represented as Moses' *spokesman*:

> And you [Moses] shall speak to him and put the words in his mouth; and I will be with your mouth and with his mouth, and will teach you what you shall do. He shall speak for you [Revised Version: He shall be thy *spokesman*] to the people; and he shall be a mouth for you, and you shall be to him as God.[2]

In the second description, Aaron is called Moses' *prophet*:

> And the LORD said to Moses, 'See, I make you as God to Pharaoh; and Aaron your brother shall be your prophet.'[3]

A prophet was a man who spoke on behalf of his god. The term was freely used for those who claimed to speak with the authority of pagan gods – like Jezebel's staff of four hundred

1. Jer. 23. 16.   2. Exod. 4. 15–16.
3. Exod. 7. 1.

and fifty prophets of Baal and four hundred prophets of Asherah, with whom Elijah contended on Mount Carmel.[1] It was also employed to describe the 'professional' Israelite prophets of the eighth and seventh centuries, whose activity and influence were so strongly deprecated by the men we now call (with dubious accuracy) the 'writing prophets'. The student of the Old Testament is faced, therefore, with the task of discriminating between the various kinds of prophet and of deciding how much more they have in common than their name and the claim to speak with divine authority which the name implies. This is a delicate undertaking and it has been made more difficult by the work of the editors from whose hands we have received the Hebrew Scriptures. In addition to introducing prophets into the historical narratives as mouthpieces of their own sermonizing,[2] they appear to have been largely responsible for giving general currency to the title 'prophet' as a description of men of God like Amos, Hosea, Isaiah, Micah, and Jeremiah, although it is questionable whether they themselves welcomed it. Whether or not any of these great figures ever explicitly repudiated the title depends upon a saying of Amos, of which the interpretation is disputed:

Then Amos answered Amaziah, 'I am no prophet, nor one of the sons of the prophets; but I am a herdsman, and a dresser of sycamore trees, and the LORD took me from following the flock, and the LORD said to me, "Go, prophesy to my people Israel." '[3]

It has been suggested that Amos here is not making a solemn pronouncement, but asking an indignant question (as though to say) 'How dare you say that I am not a true prophet because I work with the herds and sycamore trees? Don't you realize that the Lord has called me?' Other scholars prefer to read the past tense: 'I *was* no prophet, nor one of the sons of the prophets ... and the LORD said to me, "Go, prophesy to my people Israel." ' According to this latter view, Amos is claiming that his new status as a prophet rests on a divine call

1. 1 Kings 18. 19; cf. II Kings 3. 13; 10. 19.
2. Judg. 6. 7–10; 1 Sam. 2. 27–36; 1 Kings 13. 1–10; II Kings 17. 13.
3. Amos. 7. 14–15.

and not on the choice of a profession. He *was* no prophet, because he was not brought up in one of the prophetic schools.[1] It is significant that even those who deny that Amos is explicitly repudiating the title of prophet are bound to recognize that his appeal to an experience of vocation gives the title a content to which Amaziah, the sanctuary official at Bethel, was wholly unaccustomed. The kind of prophet *he* was used to was the full-time professional who made his living by giving oracles:

> And Amaziah said to Amos, 'O seer, go, flee away to the land of Judah, and eat bread there, and prophesy there; but never again prophesy at Bethel, for it is the king's sanctuary, and it is a temple of the kingdom.'[2]

Amos received this comment with indignation and his indignation is indisputable evidence that his calling was distinctive.

We are driven to the conclusion that any attempt to characterize the great prophets by defining 'prophecy' in the abstract is foredoomed to failure. Like a definition of the words 'religion' and 'priest', a definition of 'prophecy' in the Old Testament will at best lead us only to common externals which were easily identified.[3] It is precisely these features which tell us least about the great men with whom we are concerned.

THE PROFESSIONAL PROPHETS

The stature of the 'canonical' prophets stands out in bold and massive relief against the backcloth they have themselves painted of those professional prophets who claimed to announce God's will to Israel in the eighth and seventh centuries B.C.[4]

---

1. See pp. 39f., 43.
2. Amos 7. 12–13.
3. For example, the symbolic acts, which *in externals* are common to pagan and true prophet alike: 1 Kings 11. 29–31; 22. 11; Isa. 20; Jer. 13. 1–11; 19. 1–15; 27. 1–28. 17; 43. 8–13; Ezek. 4. 1–3, 4–8, 9–17; 5. 1–4; 12. 3–16, 17–20; 21. 8–17; 37. 15–28. That no *external* criteria distinguished authentic from false prophecy is clear from Jer. 28; Deut. 13. 1–5; 18. 20–2.
4. See especially: Jer. 23. 9–33; Ezek. 13.

There is a startling difference between the independence of (say) Isaiah and Jeremiah and the subservience of the professional prophets to the policy of the hour. The professional prophets were the 'yes-men' of government circles, encouraged and granted an official status, because they lent a halo of sanctity to the projects of the party in power.[1] They also made it their business to tell the ordinary citizens the 'smooth things' they delighted to hear – Ezekiel calls it 'flattering divination'[2] – and to assure them with the authority of their office that everything in the garden was lovely (proclaiming 'Peace!'), when, in fact, the state was verging on a moral and political collapse.[3] Ezekiel bitterly likens them to fools who whitewash a crumbling wall because they cannot face its ugly cracks.[4]

One of the Hebrew historians has left us a brilliant little story in I Kings 22, which reads almost as though it had been written for the specific purpose of contrasting the habitual subservience of the parasitic court-prophet with the independence of the genuine prophet of the Lord. Micaiah the son of Imlah is the hero and Zedekiah the villain of the piece. We are told how Zedekiah and his four hundred assistant prophets had been called upon to 'rubber-stamp' the joint decision of Ahab of Israel (their employer) and Jehoshaphat of Judah to undertake a military expedition against the Syrians. Their symbolic mumbo-jumbo was calculated to please Ahab (who, having paid the piper, was entitled to call the tune):

Now the king of Israel and Jehoshaphat the king of Judah were sitting on their thrones, arrayed in their robes, at the threshing floor at the entrance of the gate of Samaria; and all the prophets were prophesying before them. And Zedekiah the son of Chenaanah made for himself horns of iron, and said, 'Thus says the LORD, "With these you shall push the Syrians until they are destroyed." ' And all

1. I Kings 20. 13–15; 22. 6; II Kings 23. 2; Neh. 6. 10–14; 9. 32; cf. I Kings 18. 19.
2. Isa. 30. 10; Jer. 2. 8; 5. 31; Ezek. 12. 24; 13. 6–7.
3. Jer. 6. 14; 14. 13–16; 23. 17; 27. 14–15; 28. 9; Mic. 3. 5; Isa. 9. 15; 56. 9–12; Zech. 13. 1–6.
4. Ezek. 13. 8–16; 22. 28.

the prophets prophesied so, and said, 'Go up to Ramoth-gilead and triumph; the LORD will give it into the hand of the king.'[1]

Jehoshaphat was not the man to be satisfied with this prophetic *corps de ballet* and Zedekiah's assurances, and (to Ahab's great irritation) had asked that the prophet Micaiah should be consulted. After this request had been unwillingly accepted, we are told:

And the messenger who went to summon Micaiah said to him, 'Behold, the words of the prophets with one accord are favourable to the king; let your word be like the word of one of them, and speak favourably.'

Micaiah's reply discloses the historian's moral:

But Micaiah said, 'As the LORD lives, what the LORD says to me, that I will speak.'[2]

The great prophets' repudiation of the professional prophet seems also to be reflected in the highly sophisticated story of Balaam in Numbers 22–4. The heathen diviner, hired by Balak, king of Moab, after three unsatisfactory attempts at divination according to the regular drill, is represented as suddenly turning into a true prophet and making a stand against time-serving like that of Micaiah:

But Balaam answered and said to the servants of Balak, 'Though Balak were to give me his house full of silver and gold, I could not go beyond the command of the LORD my God, to do less or more.'[3]

It is difficult not to suspect that the story-teller is writing with knowledge of the degradation into which the professional prophets of Israel had fallen. In the time of Micah, for example, there were prophets who not only sold comforting messages to those who could pay, but 'declared war' against those who refused them money.[4] Ezekiel, similarly, preserves the memory of prophetesses who practised magic and sorcery for 'handfuls of barley and for pieces of bread'.[5] It is clear

1. 1 Kings 22. 10–12.
2. 1 Kings 22. 13–14.
3. Num. 22. 18; cf. 22. 38; 24. 13.
4. Mic. 3. 5, 11.
5. Ezek. 13. 19.

that a professional prophet's right to a fee for his services was recognized in ancient Israel,[1] but it is significant that the historian of II Kings makes a great deal of Elisha's refusal of Naaman's gift[2] and that there is never any suggestion that the canonical prophets took any sort of payment. Amos, it will be remembered, rejected with indignation Amaziah's assumption that he made his living by giving oracles. In doing so, he exposed the fundamental error of those who fail to discriminate between two radically different types of prophecy in the Old Testament.

The Word of the Lord is not communicated to men either at their own pleasure or at the convenience of their customers. Revelation comes not to order but uninvited. It is possible, therefore, to make a rough distinction between various 'prophetic' figures of the Old Testament by observing whether they offered a regular service, or whether they spoke as their conscience and the prophetic impulse demanded. In the first class, we must reckon all the prophets who made their headquarters at the court and the sanctuaries. In the second class, we must reckon the 'canonical' prophets, who, despite their close association with successive kings, always remained freelance. One of the strangest aberrations in the recent study of Israelite prophecy has been the attempt to represent men like Amos, Isaiah, and Jeremiah as differing in no important respect from the cultic prophets who operated at the sanctuaries. There is, of course, no disputing the evidence for the existence of such cultic prophets,[3] nor the fact that they are frequently associated with the sanctuary priests. So much, indeed, we may learn from Isaiah:

> These also reel with wine
>   and stagger with strong drink;
> the priest and the prophet reel with
>   strong drink,
>   they are confused with wine,
>   they stagger with strong drink;

1. I Sam. 9. 5–10; I Kings 14. 1–3; II Kings 8. 7–8.
2. II Kings 5. 19–27.
3. See, for example, I Sam. 9. 13, 22–4; 10. 5, 10; 19. 18–24; I Kings 14. 1–2; II Kings 2. 3, 5; 4. 38.

> they err in vision,
>   they stumble in giving judgement;[1]

and, again, from the book of Jeremiah:

> The priests and the prophets and all the people heard Jeremiah speaking these words in the house of the LORD. ... Then the priests and the prophets said to the princes and to all the people, 'This man deserves the sentence of death, because he has prophesied against this city, as you have heard with your own ears.'[2]

Anybody who reads Jeremiah's strictures on the prophets of Jerusalem[3] and believes that (as has been suggested) he was their colleague on the staff of the Temple is capable of self-deception to an unusual degree. We need also to be on our guard against the suggestion that the close association of priest and prophet at the sanctuaries of Israel means that the 'canonical' prophets cannot have made any radical criticisms of priestly religion. What their namesakes did does not in the least modify what they themselves said.[4]

It is obvious that the prophets who acted as professional consultants must have been proficient in some kind of technique for 'discovering' the will of God and it is equally clear that their methods associate them very closely with the old priestly religion of Canaan. Of these methods, perhaps the most naïvely mechanical were the various forms of divination and casting the sacred lot. The latter is well illustrated by Saul's use of 'Urim and Thummim' to get an answer from God: 'O LORD God of Israel, why hast thou not answered thy servant this day? If this guilt is in me or in Jonathan my son, O LORD, God of Israel, give *Urim*; but if this guilt is in thy people Israel, give *Thummim*.'[5] Nobody is quite sure what this

1. Isa. 28. 7.

2. Jer. 26. 7, 11; cf. 4. 9; 5. 30–1; 8. 1, 10; 13. 13; 14. 18; 23. 11; 27. 16; 29. 1; 35. 4; Lam. 2. 20; 4. 13; Hos. 4. 4–8; Mic. 3. 11; Zeph. 3. 4. It is possible that the cultic prophets were ultimately reduced to the status of singing men in the choir of the Second Temple; compare II Kings 23. 2 and II Chron. 34. 30; cf. I Chron. 25. 1–8; II Chron. 20. 1–30.

3. Jer. 2. 8; 5. 30–1; 6. 13–14; 8. 10–11; 14. 13–15; 18. 18; 23. 9–40; 26. 8, 11, 16; 27. 1–28. 16.

4. See pp. 109–14.

5. I Sam. 14. 41; cf. I Sam. 23. 9–12; 28. 6; 30. 7–8; Ezek. 13. 6–7; Deut. 33. 8; Num. 27. 21.

device was exactly, but it is probable that marked stones were used of which the interpretation was settled beforehand, as when we toss a coin. We need go no further than the evidence supplied by the Old Testament itself to recognize that divination, so far from being peculiar to the Hebrews, was a favourite pagan method of obtaining a divine ruling.[1] It is not surprising, therefore, that men like Micah and Jeremiah should have vehemently opposed the prophets who practised divination and that there should be ancient laws in line with the prophets' protest.[2]

Human beings have always been susceptible to communications represented as having been received in a state of ecstatic trance. Many bogus types of 'spiritualism' exploit our credulity even today, very much as the professional prophets of Israel (literally) 'cashed in' on the gullibility of their contemporaries in the eighth and seventh centuries B.C. A scathing comment from Isaiah on the prophets who 'err in vision' through wine and strong drink suggests one possible source of their inspiration.[3] Another stimulus was music, which, it seems, both induced and controlled 'spirit-possession'.[4] Saul, again, provides the illustration. He is told by Samuel that he will 'meet a band of prophets coming down from the high place with harp, tambourine, flute, and lyre before them, prophesying. Then the spirit of the LORD will come mightily upon you, and you shall prophesy with them and be turned into another man.'[5] It is hardly surprising that prophecy could be regarded as being synonymous with lunacy.[6] Evidently, there were prophets in Israel whose behaviour was not dissimilar from the frantic raving of Jezebel's prophets of Baal, who 'cried aloud, and cut themselves after

1. Num. 22. 7; 1 Sam. 6. 2; Isa. 44. 25; 47. 12–13; Ezek. 21. 21.
2. Mic. 3. 11; Jer. 14. 14; 27. 9; 29. 8; Isa. 3. 2–3; Ezek. 13. 6–7, 23; Zech. 10. 2; 1 Sam. 15. 23; 28. 3; II Kings 17. 17; 21. 6; Deut. 18. 10; Lev. 19. 26; 20. 6, 27.
3. Isa. 28. 7; cf. Mic. 2. 11.
4. 1 Sam. 16. 14–23; 18. 10–11; 19. 9; cf. II Kings 3. 15; 1 Chron. 25. 1–2; Exod. 15. 20–1.
5. 1 Sam. 10. 5–6.
6. Jer. 29. 26; Hos. 9. 7; 1 Sam. 19. 23–4; cf. II Kings 9. 11; Zech. 13. 1–6.

their custom with swords and lances, until the blood gushed out upon them. And as midday passed, they raved on until the time of the offering of the oblation, but there was no voice; no one answered, no one heeded.'[1] The canonical prophets are never found employing artificial stimuli and before the Exile usually avoid attributing their oracles to the 'spirit of God'.[2] They prefer to use terms which are less ambiguous, like 'the hand of the LORD'.[3]

Dreams represent another of the media by which the professional soothsayer claimed to receive divine intelligence. They appear to have been acknowledged for a time by one school of Old Testament writers as a valid means of revelation,[4] but Jeremiah makes it quite clear that he has no use for them:

> I have heard what the prophets have said who prophesy lies in my name, saying, 'I have dreamed, I have dreamed!' How long shall there be lies in the heart of the prophets who prophesy lies, and who prophesy the deceit of their own heart, who think to make my people forget my name by their dreams which they tell one another, even as their fathers forgot my name for Baal? Let the prophet who has a dream tell the dream, but let him who has my word speak my word faithfully. What has *straw* in common with *wheat*? says the LORD.[5]

Straw and wheat is an admirable summary of the relationship between the professional prophets and Israel's great men of God. Their difference in quality makes it difficult to appreciate their common root. All the evidence which the student accumulates to demonstrate the great prophets' emergence from some lower type in a postulated evolutionary scale (early diviner, primitive ecstatic, or cultic official) in the end turns to mock him by throwing into still bolder relief their incomparable quality. The problem of the historical antecedents of eighth-century Hebrew prophecy is that of tracing the central Israelite tradition which stemmed from Moses and it is in-

1. 1 Kings 18. 28–9.
2. Mic. 3. 8 probably reflects a post-exilic outlook; cf. Num. 11. 29; Joel 2. 28; Ezek. 11. 5; Isa. 61. 1; II Chron. 20. 14–15; 24. 20.
3. Isa. 8. 11; cf. Ezek. 1. 3; 3. 14; 8. 1; 37. 1; I Kings 18. 46.
4. Gen. 20. 3; 40. 5–8; 41. 9–13; I Kings 3. 5.
5. Jer. 23. 25–8; cf. 27. 9; 29. 8; Zech. 10. 2; Deut. 13. 1–3.

soluble, because our records simply do not supply the necessary evidence. There is, however, a most suggestive collection of stories in the books of Kings,[1] which, if they cannot be said to bridge the gap between Moses and Amos, at least establish the existence (about 850 B.C.) of what has been wittily labelled *Mosaic*, as distinct from *Amos*aic, prophecy.[2] The dominant figure of these stories is the prophet Elijah. All we know about him has been preserved in a popular tradition, of which, presumably, his successor Elisha may be taken as being fairly representative. The prophetic communities – the 'sons of the prophets' – over which Elisha presided[3] are probably responsible for claiming for their master a 'double share' of Elijah's spirit[4] and what that meant for them is clear from the miracle-working they have ascribed to him.[5] Although their love of the miraculous has also coloured the accounts of Elijah,[6] he emerges, nevertheless, as a gaunt desert figure of forbidding appearance and fierce conviction[7] – a worthy successor to Moses and a convincing forerunner of Amos. Although none of his oracles has been preserved, this 'Troubler of Israel'[8] had clearly stood in the Council of God[9] and heard his word.[10] His prophetic zeal symbolizes and expresses the distinctiveness of Israel's faith:

I have been very jealous for the LORD, the God of hosts; for the people of Israel have forsaken thy covenant, thrown down thy altars, and slain thy prophets with the sword; and I, even I only, am left; and they seek my life, to take it away.[11]

In the ninth century B.C., the faith of Israel was seriously

1. The stories of Elijah: I Kings 17–19; 21; II Kings 1–2; the stories of Elisha: I Kings 19. 19–21; II Kings 2–7; 8. 1–15; 9. 1–13; 13. 14–21.
2. Notice the references to the 'prophets of the Lord': I Kings 18. 4, 22; 19. 10.
3. II Kings 2. 3, 5; 4. 1, 38; 6. 1–4; 9. 1; see, further, pp. 35f., 39f.
4. II Kings 2. 9.
5. II Kings 2. 19–22, 23–5; 4. 1–7, 11–37, 38–41; 6. 4–7; 13. 14–19.
6. I Kings 17. 8–16, 17–24; 19. 5–8.
7. II Kings 1. 8; I Kings 18. 46.
8. I Kings 18. 17; cf. 21. 20.
9. I Kings 17. 1; 18. 15; see pp. 45f.
10. I Kings 17. 2, 8; 18. 36; 19. 9; II Kings 10. 17.
11. I Kings 19. 10.

imperilled by the old Canaanite religion of Palestine,[1] forti-
fied, as it was, in Ahab's reign (about 871–852 B.C.) by the
establishment of a Baal cult at the behest of the Tyrian Jezebel, his notorious and domineering wife.[2] Elijah's contest on
Mount Carmel with the court prophets of Baal[3] epitomizes
the battle which rages through the history of Israelite prophecy to the time of the Exile. Elijah's uncompromising demand
for a decision between the God of Israel and Baal strikes the
authentic note of prophecy:

'How long will you go limping with two different opinions? If the
LORD is God, follow him; but if Baal, then follow him.' And the
people did not answer him a word.[4]

The inspiration of this decisive vigour, which is seen again in
Elijah's defiance of Jezebel's covetous intrigues to get possession of Naboth's vineyard,[5] is wonderfully presented in the
account of the prophet's experience on Horeb, the Mount of
God:

And behold, the LORD passed by, and a great and strong wind rent
the mountains, and broke in pieces the rocks before the LORD, but
the LORD was not in the wind; and after the wind an earthquake,
but the LORD was not in the earthquake; and after the earthquake a
fire, but the LORD was not in the fire; and after the fire a still small
voice. And when Elijah heard it, he wrapped his face in his mantle
and went out and stood at the entrance of the cave.[6]

The God who discloses himself to Elijah is none other than
the God of Moses; we are clearly intended to recognize the
significance of the Mount of Revelation.[7] At the same time,
the emphasis falls on a highly significant difference. God's
revelation is now more markedly personal, not thundered
but whispered. This emphasis on revelation as *personal* is a
characteristic feature of the great pre-exilic prophets and no
doubt it represents a genuine development in the Israelite
tradition. We must not allow our repudiation of the myth of
inevitable progress to prevent our recognizing the emergence

1. 1 Kings 18. 17–19; II Kings 1. 2–3; see pp. 71f.
2. 1 Kings 16. 29–33.   3. 1 Kings 18. 17–40.
4. 1 Kings 18. 21.   5. 1 Kings 21; see pp. 105f.
6. 1 Kings 19. 11–13.   7. Exod. 3. 1–6; 19. 16–25.

of authentically new insight within the stream of tradition. Elijah points forward as well as back. The 'still small voice' which he heard prepares us for an understanding of prophecy by which Moses himself came to be described as the friend of God.

THE FRIENDS OF GOD

There is a remarkable passage in the book of Numbers which illuminates the two contrasted types of prophet we have been considering:

> Hear my words: If there is a prophet among you, I the LORD make myself known to him in a vision, I speak with him in a dream. Not so with my servant Moses; he is entrusted with all my house. With him I speak mouth to mouth, clearly, and not in dark speech; and he beholds the form of the LORD.[1]

Alongside this, we may set one of those telling Hebrew similes, which often by their very daring make the matter plain:

> Thus the LORD used to speak to Moses face to face, *as a man speaks to his friend.*[2]

The canonical prophets of Israel stand in the tradition of Moses and (as we shall see later) it is to the austere community of the desert that we must trace their spiritual ancestry. Like Moses, they were men who had been admitted to God's intimate circle and taken into his confidence.[3]

Jeremiah is the most explicit of the prophets in affirming that such direct personal knowledge of God is the fundamental ground of true prophetic authority. He sums up his conviction in a wonderfully suggestive word (*sôdh*), which is translated 'council', in his diagnosis of the failure of the professional prophets:

> For who among them has stood in
> the council of the LORD
> to perceive and to hear his word,
> or who has given heed to his word
> and listened?

1. Num. 12. 6–8.
2. Exod. 33. 11; cf. Wisdom of Solomon 7. 27.
3. Deut. 18. 15; 34. 10; Hos. 12. 13.

I did not send the prophets,
    yet they ran;
I did not speak to them,
    yet they prophesied.

But if they had stood in my council,
    then they would have proclaimed
        my words to my people,
and they would have turned them
        from their evil way,
    and from the evil of their doings.[1]

The significance of the word *ṣôdh* may be judged from the
other Old Testament passages in which it is used. We find that
it means, for instance, a friendly group of young men who
enjoy each other's company and (as the Psalmist puts it) take
'sweet counsel' together.[2] It is also used of the secrets
of intimate acquaintances, or of conspirators, who are as
'thick as thieves';[3] and, most significantly, it describes God's
'covenant-friendship' with those who practise true religion:

The friendship (*ṣôdh*) of the LORD is for
    those who fear him,
and he makes known to them his covenant.[4]

The prophets had been admitted into the intimate fellowship of God's Heavenly Council – a characteristically concrete Hebrew conception, which is frequently reflected in the
Old Testament.[5] For this reason, they were able to hear and
proclaim the counsel of the Lord:

Surely the Lord GOD does nothing,
    without revealing his secret (*ṣôdh*)
    to his servants the prophets.[6]

It must always be something of an impertinence to attempt
to stretch any sort of spiritual experience on the rack of our

1. Jer. 23. 18, 21–2.
2. Ps. 55. 14; cf. Jer. 6. 11; 15. 17.
3. Prov. 11. 13; 20. 19; 25. 9; Ps. 64. 2.
4. Ps. 25. 14.
5. Job 1. 1–2. 13; 15. 8; Pss. 82; 89. 7; 1 Kings 22. 19–22.
6. Amos 3. 7; cf. Isa. 6. 8.

psychological categories and this is even more obviously true in the case of the great prophets, of whose inner consciousness our evidence is no less slight than our ability to interpret it. The significant discovery we make as we read the prophetic writings is that the really great men of God did not wear their heart on their sleeve for all to examine. They leave preoccupation with the *mechanism* of religion to lesser mortals. Like all the Hebrews, they knew nothing of our dubious distinction between 'subjective' and 'objective' experience, just as we know little of their ability to embrace the material and spiritual worlds in a profound unity, so that mundane physical experience could become vibrant with spiritual significance. This meant that the everyday life of the prophets was always potentially a manifestation of God's will and that very little was needed to strike them into making specific utterances.[1] For example, in the first chapter of Jeremiah, we read:

And the word of the LORD came to me, saying, 'Jeremiah, what do you see?' And I said, 'I see a rod of *almond*.' Then the LORD said to me, 'You have seen well, for I am *watching* over my word to perform it.'[2]

As the marginal reading in our translations indicates, the words italicized represent two very similar Hebrew words – *shāqēdh* (almond) and *shōqēdh* (watching). The sight of an almond tree and the sound of its name brought to articulate expression the prophet's knowledge of God's 'wakefulness'. Similarly, when Amos saw a basket of summer fruit, the word for summer fruit (*qáyiç*) released his prophetic conviction that Israel was doomed and approaching her end (*qēç*).[3] The apparent triviality of this chance association is in startling contrast with the elaborate devices employed by the professional prophets when they wished to obtain an oracle.

Just as the great prophets did not differentiate between spiritual and physical experience, so they did not separate what we should call their religious and their moral experience. The concern of the prophets with moral issues would lead us to expect that an urge to prophesy often came as a result of the

1. See Jer. 1. 13–14 (the boiling cauldron); 18. 1–4 (the potter); 24. 1–3 (the two baskets of figs).
2. Jer. 1. 11–12.   3. Amos 8. 1–2.

demands of their conscience. If we are looking for mechanisms in terms of which we may explain the authority of the prophets, the significance of their moral discrimination will escape us. If, however, we are prepared to acknowledge that 'value-judgement' is one of the ways of knowing God, we shall attach the greatest importance to the hint given in Jeremiah:

> Therefore thus says the LORD:
> 'If you return, I will restore you,
>   and you shall stand before me.
> If you utter what is precious, and
>   not what is worthless,
>   you shall be as my mouth.'[1]

Here the prophet is called upon to acknowledge his own defection from God and repent of his self-pity. Only by the discrimination which flows from a heightened personal awareness can he discharge his prophetic office. Again, we notice the gulf which separates the corybantic seer and the true man of God.

If the inner core of the prophetic consciousness is this intensified spiritual-and-moral awareness, we must expect to fail in all our clumsy attempts to split up into their constituent elements the visionary experiences which the prophets record. Their simple introductions – 'Thus the Lord GOD showed me,' 'I saw the Lord,' and 'Jeremiah, what do you see?'[2] – suggest a direct communion with God, very different from both the almost pathological behaviour of some of the professional prophets and the stylized visions of (say) Zechariah, which, without the services of an interpreting angel, are enigmatic 'dark speeches'.[3] In the vast bulk of prophetic utterances after Second Isaiah, the medium is more in evidence and much of the old immediacy has disappeared.

There is always a danger of our being tempted to degrade the consciousness of the prophets to the impersonal level, in order (as we falsely suppose) to safeguard the objective authority of their oracles (how in all religious matters we pursue the mirage of objectivity and delight to define authority in

---

1. Jer. 15. 19.   2. Amos 7. 1, 4, 7; 8. 1; 9. 1; Isa. 6. 1; Jer. 1. 11.
3. Zech. 1. 9, 19; cf. Ezek. 40. 3–4. See p. 24 n. 1.

terms external to human awareness and response!). That such an insensitive procedure is unnecessary is well demonstrated by the fragments we possess of Jeremiah's spiritual diary. It contains one of the most shattering passages in the Bible:

> Cursed be the day
>   on which I was born!
> The day when my mother bore me,
>   let it not be blessed!
> Cursed be the man
>   who brought the news to my father,
> 'A son is born to you,'
>   making him very glad.
> Let that man be like the cities
>   which the LORD overthrew without pity;
> let him hear a cry in the morning
>   and an alarm at noon,
> because he did not kill me in the womb;
>   so my mother would have been my grave,
>   and her womb for ever great.
> Why did I come forth from the womb
>   to see toil and sorrow,
>   and spend my days in shame?[1]

This terrible cry of dereliction – like that other cry from a cross of suffering six hundred years later – is not a denial of the prophet's vocation, but the very strongest confirmation of its depth. Jeremiah had accepted the office of being God's spokesman to the nation, but not only that; he had also undertaken to bear in his own life the burden of God's grief at his people's sin. Hosea before him had suffered the conflict between the love which must express itself in judgement and the love which demands mercy, and had boldly identified his own pathos with the pathos of God himself:

> How can I give you up, O Ephraim!
>   How can I hand you over, O Israel!
> My heart recoils within me,
>   my compassion grows warm and tender.[2]

1. Jer. 20. 14–18; cf. Job. 3.   2. Hos. 11. 8.

A large part of Jeremiah's spiritual anguish sprang from his recognition that he was 'out of tune' with God. There were occasions when he became conscience-stricken with the fear that the zeal of his denunciations had outstripped in austerity the righteous love of God for his people.[1] And there were times when his human sympathy pleaded for pity and almost persuaded him to give in and relinquish his mission. A teacher of human wisdom may decide to retire, but not so a prophet:

> If I say, 'I will not mention him,
>   or speak any more in his name,'
> there is in my heart as it were a burning fire
>   shut up in my bones,
> and I am weary with holding it in,
>   and I cannot.[2]

It was of this same moral and spiritual compulsion that Amos spoke in one of the few hints he has left us of his inner sense of vocation:

> The Lord GOD has spoken;
>   who can but prophesy?[3]

Jeremiah proved the intense reality of his prophetic vocation by faithfulness not only in private spiritual agony, but also in a public life of isolation and persecution. His divine commission won for him the hostility of his family and the ostracism of his familiar friends. It meant sacrificing the possibility of marriage and of a happy family life and this was a self-denial which we perhaps can hardly appreciate to the full in the modern world of the West.[4] The friendship of God was indeed a costly privilege:

> But I was like a gentle lamb
>   led to the slaughter.
> I did not know it was against me
>   they devised schemes, saying,
> 'Let us destroy the tree with its fruit,
>   let us cut him off from the land of the living,
>   that his name be remembered no more.'[5]

1. Jer. 17. 14–18. 2. Jer. 20. 9; cf. 5. 14; 6. 11.
3. Amos 3. 8; cf. Isa. 8. 11; Ezek. 3. 14.
4. Jer. 16. 1–2; 15. 10–21; 18. 18–23; 20. 1–6; 26. 7–19; 32. 2–5; 36. 5; 37. 16–21; 38. 1–13. 5. Jer. 11. 19.

We are inevitably reminded of the Servant of the Lord in Second Isaiah, whose experience corresponded so closely to that of Jeremiah that some scholars have found in the likeness a clue to the baffling problem of the Servant's identity:

> He was oppressed, and he was afflicted,
> yet he opened not his mouth;
> like a lamb that is led to the slaughter,
> and like a sheep that before its
> shearers is dumb,
> so he opened not his mouth.[1]

The outstanding feature in this recorded experience is its personal dedication. Here is the proof, if proof be needed, that the great prophets were servants in God's household and not mere tools in his hands. Their personalities were neither dissolved by fusion with the divine in any sort of 'mystic union', not yet swept aside by the violence of any non-moral ecstatic afflatus.[2] When they were commissioned as 'men of God', they remained *men* – and that is why they can so powerfully mediate to human persons the self-disclosure of the personal God. If, then, we wish to speak of the compelling power of God with which the prophetic oracles surge, we must remember that it was the deepest kind of compulsion – that which is known in personal communion and grounded in moral conviction.

This conclusion about the source of the astonishing urgency of the prophets' teaching is confirmed by the accounts they have left us of their 'calls' to the prophetic ministry.[3] Significantly, they are usually cast in the form of a dialogue with God in which it is he who takes the initiative.

These men were not born to a profession; they did not pass through a novitiate or join any prophetic guild; nor did they submit themselves to a course of theological instruction. They

1. Isa. 53. 7.
2. The point is well illustrated by Jer. 42. 7, which suggests that the prophet meditated for no less than ten days before speaking in God's name. A similar interval is mentioned in Jer. 28. 11–12.
3. Amos 7. 14–15; Isa. 6; Jer. 1. 4–10; Ezek. 1. 1–3. 27; Exod. 3–4; 1 Sam. 3; cf. Isa. 42. 1–4; 49. 1–6.

finished as they began – laymen. Amos (like Elisha) was working in the fields when the 'call' came:

the LORD took me from following the flock, and the LORD said to
me, 'Go, prophesy to my people Israel.'[1]

The simplicity of this statement is self-authenticating. Moses,
similarly, was tending his father-in-law's flock when he saw
the vision in the Burning Bush; the account of it in Exodus
corresponds closely in form to that of Isaiah, although the
latter received his call in the Temple.[2] Jeremiah and the
Servant of the Lord (like St Paul) expressed the certainty they
felt about their vocation, by describing it as a mission to which
they were destined before birth:

> Before I formed you in the womb
>   I knew you,
> and before you were born I consecrated you;
> I appointed you a prophet to the nations.[3]

Incredulity and a feeling of weakness appear to have been
the common human reaction to God's communication of his
purpose. The exquisite confession of Jeremiah – 'Ah, Lord
GOD! Behold, I do not know how to speak, for I am only a
youth' – is echoed in the words attributed to Moses:

Oh, my Lord, I am not eloquent, either heretofore or since thou
hast spoken to thy servant; but I am slow of speech and of tongue.[4]

How very different this is from the brazen self-confidence of
the professional soothsayer! The drama of Isaiah's vision develops rather differently. Israel's desperate need of the prophetic ministry is first made plain by a contrast between the
abundant worth of God (his 'glory') and the wretched un-
worthiness of his people as represented by Isaiah himself. This
contrast so penetrated the prophet's innermost being that it
provoked the classic confession:

1. Amos 7. 15; I Kings 19. 19–21; cf. II Sam. 7. 8–9.
2. Exod. 3. 1–6; Isa. 6.
3. Jer. 1. 5; cf. Isa. 49. 1, 5; Galatians 1. 15.
4. Exod. 4. 10; cf. Jer. 1. 6; Exod. 6. 12; Judg. 6. 15.

Woe is me! For I am lost; for I am a man of unclean lips, and I dwell in the midst of a people of unclean lips; for my eyes have seen the King, the LORD of hosts![1]

In each case, God makes a demand which is insupportable without his succour. Therefore a promise of his presence follows:

But I will be with you. ...Now therefore go, and I will be with your mouth and teach you what you shall speak.[2]

This promise is sometimes made specific for the individual prophet by a symbolic touch, as in the call of Jeremiah:

Then the LORD put forth his hand and touched my mouth; and the LORD said to me,
'Behold, I have put my words in your mouth.'[3]

The same conviction is represented in Isaiah by the image of the altar stone which touched the prophet's lips, and in Ezekiel by the symbolic eating of the double-sided roll of oracles.

In all these accounts, there is the explicit recognition that the prophet's mission will be accomplished only in the teeth of a powerful opposition. This may even deny the prophet's authority:

Then Moses answered, 'But behold, they will not believe me or listen to my voice, for they will say, "The LORD did not appear to you." '[4]

Nevertheless, the message must be proclaimed – 'whether they hear, or refuse to hear.'[5] That it might ultimately fail to awaken a response is reflected – with that lack of discrimination between purpose and result so characteristic of Hebrew thought and so perplexing to us[6] – in the conclusion of Isaiah's initial vision. The prophet is commissioned (apparently) only to confirm the nation in its moral and spiritual lethargy:

1. Isa. 6. 5; compare the vision of Ezek. 1. 4–28.
2. Exod. 3. 12 and 4. 12; cf. Jer. 15. 19; Judg. 6. 16, 22–3.
3. Jer. 1. 9; cf. Isa. 6. 7; Ezek. 2. 8–3. 3; 1 Sam. 3. 19.
4. Exod. 4. 1; cf. Jer. 1. 8; 1 Sam. 3. 11; Ezek. 3. 4–9.
5. Ezek. 2. 7.
6. See, for example, Hos. 8. 4; Hab. 2. 10; Isa. 30. 1; 44. 9; Jer. 7. 18.

And he said, 'Go, and say to this people:
    "Hear and hear, but do not understand;
    see and see, but do not perceive."
Make the heart of this people fat,
    and their ears heavy,
    and shut their eyes;
lest they see with their eyes,
    and hear with their ears,
and understand with their hearts,
    and turn and be healed.'[1]

Again, we notice what a difference there is between this moral seriousness and the easy optimism of the professional prophet.

We cannot penetrate further than these confessions take us into the secret of the utter conviction which informs the life and preaching of all the great prophets. Their knowledge of God was too deep and personal to be compatible with any kind of religiosity. It is therefore not surprising that they describe their initial and vital religious experience in the modest form of a conversation with God in the context of their everyday pursuits. It was enough for them that God spoke to them through the life with which they were familiar, by giving it a new dimension – that of himself, his love and his righteousness. This new dimension revealed the divine purpose; and that compelled their utterance.

1. Isa. 6. 9–10.

CHAPTER THREE

THE VOCATION OF THE PEOPLE

For all their splendid individuality, for all their courage in bearing the burden of isolation, the Hebrew prophets never withdrew from their primary and public function of being the Lord's 'watchmen over Israel,' his spokesmen – not to this or that individual, but to the nation at large.[1] It is possible to present a great part of their teaching in terms of their conception of Israel, since all their efforts were devoted to the task of making the nation a people fit for God's own possession and purpose. In other words, the prophets expressed their convictions about the nature of God in terms of their convictions about the true vocation and destiny of Israel. The question 'What is Israel?' is therefore one of the fundamental questions which every reader of the prophetic books must always have in the forefront of his mind.

THE ISRAELITE TRADITION

It is very tempting for us to think of Israel in terms of the nation-states we know in our own world. Israel then becomes simply the kingdom founded by Saul about three thousand years ago, and later extinguished – in part by Assyria's invasion of the northern kingdom in 721 B.C. and wholly by Babylon's conquest of the southern kingdom in 586 B.C. This political view, however, is entirely foreign to all the Old Testament writers, who are unanimous in their conviction that the true Israel was essentially a people in communion with God. The People of God neither began with the reign of Saul nor came to an end with the catastrophe of the Exile. Indeed, it is the community of which Christians believe themselves to be members in the twentieth century. To ask when it came into being is therefore no merely antiquarian

1. Jer. 6. 17; Ezek. 3. 17; 33. 2, 7; Hab. 2. 1; Hos. 9. 8; Isa. 56. 10.

question. It is an inquiry into God's purpose and method in the biggest possible sense.

The Exodus Tradition

If we are tempted to suppose that the People of God was an abstract religious idea which the prophets invented for themselves, the evidence of their teaching will come as a surprise. With impressive unanimity,[1] they affirm that Israel was brought into being by God, when (probably about 1250 B.C.) he brought their enslaved forefathers out of Egypt. Nothing could be more explicit than the declaration of Amos:

> Also I brought you up out of the land of Egypt,
> > and led you forty years in the wilderness,
> > to possess the land of the Amorite.[2]

Hosea, similarly, begins his tender picture of God's 'adoption' of his people with the words:

> When Israel was a child, I loved him,
> > and out of Egypt I called my son.[3]

It is tempting to multiply evidence of the Exodus tradition in the prophetic writings,[4] but the following oracle from Jeremiah must suffice. He likens the creation of Israel to a marriage and contrasts her loyalty during the early days of the honeymoon with her infidelity once she had settled down in Palestine:

> I remember the devotion of your youth,
> > your love as a bride,
> how you followed me in the wilderness,
> > in a land not sown.

> Israel was holy to the LORD
> > the first fruits of his harvest.
> All who ate of it became guilty;
> > evil came upon them ...

1. Isaiah is the odd man out; see p. 158.
2. Amos 2. 10; cf. 3. 1; 9. 7.
3. Hos. 11. 1; cf. 12. 9; 13. 4; Exod. 4. 22; Jer. 31. 9, 20.
4. Jer. 11. 1–5; 15. 1–2; 16. 14–15; 23. 7–8; 31. 31–4; Ezek. 20. 5–6; Mic. 6. 4; Mal. 4. 4; see also pp. 58, 118.

What wrong did your fathers find in me
>that they went far from me,
and went after worthlessness, and became worthless?

They did not say, 'Where is the LORD
>who brought us up from the land of Egypt,
who led us in the wilderness,
>in a land of deserts and pits,
in a land of drought and deep darkness,
>in a land that none passes through,
>where no man dwells?'

And I brought you into a plentiful land
>to enjoy its fruits and its good things.
But when you came in you defiled my land,
>and made my heritage an abomination.[1]

It is clear that for the great prophets 'Israel' was not an idea or even an ideal, but a fact of history, brought into being through an event in which God disclosed his gracious purpose. Their interpretation of the Exodus as having this momentous significance was part of the debt they owed to a tradition founded by Moses, the first of the prophets. Although we cannot document this tradition from any genuinely Mosaic writings, the book Deuteronomy has preserved an ancient creed which long continued to be recited at the offering of first-fruits at the sanctuary. Its terms are of great interest:

A wandering Aramean was my father; and he went down into Egypt and sojourned there, few in number; and there he became a nation, great, mighty, and populous. And the Egyptians treated us harshly, and afflicted us, and laid upon us hard bondage. Then we cried to the LORD the God of our fathers, and the LORD heard our voice, and saw our affliction, our toil, and our oppression; and the LORD brought us out of Egypt with a mighty hand and an out-stretched arm, with great terror, with signs and wonders; and he brought us into this place and gave us this land, a land flowing with milk and honey.[2]

If, as some judge, this confession goes back to the period of the conquest of Palestine (about 1250–1020 B.C.), we are

1. Jer. 2. 2–3, 5–7.
2. Deut. 26. 5–9. A similar creed will be found in Deut. 6. 20–5.

justified in emphasizing not only the religious experience of the prophets, but also their *historic* faith.

The Patriarchal Tradition

'I am the LORD your God from the land of Egypt'[1] is, as we have just seen, the core of the faith of the great pre-exilic prophets. For them, Israel was the People of the God of the Exodus. While this affirmation remains the dominant emphasis of the Old Testament as a whole,[2] outside the pre-exilic prophets, it is supplemented by a further tradition, which identifies the call of Israel with the call of Abraham. Thus Second Isaiah presses back the origin of Israel to the first Hebrew:

> Hearken to me, you who pursue deliverance,
>   you who seek the LORD;
> look to the rock from which you were hewn,
>   and to the quarry from which you were digged.
> Look to Abraham your father
>   and to Sarah who bore you;
> for when he was but one I called him,
>   and I blessed him and made him many.[3]

The difficulty we find in trying to combine this patriarchal tradition with that of the Exodus is only a reflection of the difficulty actually experienced by the Israelites in history of trying to combine in one people the various tribes who had infiltrated into Palestine before the Exodus and never taken part in it with the main body of Israelites who entered Palestine after their deliverance from Egypt. It is probable that the story of the covenant at Shechem in the last chapter of the book of Joshua records the admission of some of the first group into the main Israelite body. This would account for the combination in Joshua's speech on that occasion of the tradition

---

1. Hos. 12. 9; cf. Exod. 20. 2. The Passover celebrated the deliverance from Egypt: Deut. 16. 1–8.
2. See, for example, Pss. 66. 6; 78; 136. 10–16.
3. Isa. 51. 1–2; cf. 29. 22; 41. 8–10; 63. 16; Mic. 7. 20; Ezek. 33. 24; Ps. 105. 6, 42.

of Abraham and the patriarchs with the tradition of Moses and the Exodus:

> Your fathers lived of old beyond the Euphrates, Terah, the father of Abraham and of Nahor; and they served other gods. Then I took your father Abraham from beyond the River and led him through all the land of Canaan, and made his offspring many. I gave him Isaac; and to Isaac I gave Jacob and Esau. And I gave Esau the hill country of Seir to possess, but Jacob and his children went down to Egypt. And I sent Moses and Aaron, and I plagued Egypt with what I did in the midst of it; and afterwards I brought you out ... and you lived in the wilderness a long time. Then I brought you to the land of the Amorites ... and you took possession of their land, and I destroyed them before you.[1]

You can see at a glance that this credal confession with its three focal points – (*a*) the call of Abraham, (*b*) the deliverance at the Exodus, and (*c*) the gift of Palestine – summarizes the ground covered in the first six books of the Bible (Genesis–Joshua). Whatever the authenticity of the patriarchal narratives as history (and archaeological discoveries have shown that at least they reflect with accuracy the general movements and conditions of the turbulent period they depict), it is evident that they have been geared to the normative Exodus tradition and made to look forward to the deliverance from Egypt. That great act of redemption becomes, therefore, the fulfilment of the promise made to Abraham and his seed:

> Now the LORD said to Abram, 'Go from your country and your kindred and your father's house to the land that I will show you. And I will make of you a great nation ... and by you all the families of the earth will bless themselves.'[2]

The significance of God's redemptive self-disclosure in the People of God for *all the families of the earth*[3] is expounded in the parables of Genesis 2–11. They constitute a kind of prologue to the main epic of God's redemption, which starts in Genesis 12, and present the plight of all mankind, created by God and yet in rebellion against him, to which the call of Abraham is

---

1. Josh. 24. 2–5, 7–8.
2. Gen. 12. 1–3; cf. 26. 24 (Isaac); 28. 13–15 (Jacob).
3. See Gen. 22. 18; 26. 4; 28. 14.

the beginning of the answer. Through his servant Israel, God, the Creator of all men, draws near as their Redeemer. It is precisely this profound conviction about the universal meaning of Israel's vocation, first writ large in Genesis and Exodus, that Second Isaiah takes up and brings to consummate expression:

> Thus says God, the LORD,
>   who created the heavens and stretched them out,
>   who spread forth the earth and what comes from it,
> who gives breath to the people upon it
>   and spirit to those who walk in it:
> 'I am the LORD, I have called you in righteousness,
>   I have taken you by the hand and kept you;
> I have given you as a covenant to the people,
>   a light to the nations,
>   to open the eyes that are blind,
> to bring out the prisoners from the dungeon,
>   from the prison those who sit in darkness.'[1]

We are again forced to the conclusion that the great prophets are not adequately described as innovators; they were also inheritors of the ancestral faith of their people. Their impact is revolutionary, because the tradition which they received was set aflame in the unprecedented intensity of their religious experience, and there purged of all those elements which stood in the way of personal communion with the God who had called them.

The Prophetic Insight

The prophetic conception of Israel is, as we have seen, indissolubly bound up with the work of Moses. It was Moses who inspired a group of dispirited tribesmen to risk everything in dependence on his God. The Old Testament echoes and re-echoes with the joyful recognition of this supreme moment in Hebrew history, but, like all great moments in history, it has not escaped misinterpretation by well-meaning but pedestrian minds. And so it comes about that Moses, the prophetic man of God who responded to God's self-disclosure,

1. Isa. 42. 5–7.

is now represented as the law-giver *par excellence* and concealed behind huge blocks of priestly legislation amassed in the post-exilic period. These are not appropriate monuments to the work he accomplished – or, to speak more accurately, to the work God accomplished through him – as the prophets saw it.

If we glance rapidly at the passages in the prophetic writings which refer to the birth of Israel in Egypt, we notice immediately that they differ in emphasis from the many other accounts of the Exodus tradition in the Old Testament. They contain, for instance, no suggestion that it was the giving of the Law at Sinai which endowed Israel with her special identity (even though, as many scholars now believe, the Ten Commandments of Exodus 20 may come from Moses himself). Nor do they contain any suggestion that the 'covenant' between God and his people was a legal agreement sealed by a formal act of sacrifice. What did arouse the prophets' unceasing wonder and praise was the personal and moral bond which God then established between Israel and himself. God had admitted the prophets into the essential relationship which constituted the reality of his people's vocation. Israel had been chosen as they had been chosen.[1] In the immediacy of their awareness, Israel was known to be a prophetic community with all the privileges and responsibilities of a prophetic vocation. That is the basic faith of the Old Testament on which all else is commentary.

Nothing is more striking than the way in which the prophets' conception of Israel's calling corresponds, feature by feature, with their own personal sense of vocation. It is found at its most explicit in the following oracle of Second Isaiah:

> But you, Israel, my servant,
>   Jacob, whom I have chosen,
>   the offspring of Abraham, my friend;
> you whom I took from the ends of the earth,
>   and called from its farthest corners,
> saying to you, 'You are my servant,
>   I have chosen you and not cast you off';
>   fear not, for I am with you,

1. The conviction that Israel was an elect people is expressed with great emphasis in Deut. 4. 37; 7. 6–8; 10. 15; 14. 2.

be not dismayed, for I am your God;
I will strengthen you, I will help you,
I will uphold you with my victorious right hand.[1]

We saw in the last chapter how the great prophets described their assurance of God's presence and sustaining power in almost identical terms.[2]

The metaphorical description of Israel as God's 'servant' illuminates this correspondence between the vocation of people and prophet. The patriarchs, as the fathers of Israel, are called the Lord's servants,[3] as are the members of his chosen people.[4] The term is often used of Moses, through whom the prophetic community was called into being.[5] It is also frequently applied to the prophets[6] and in some of the oracles of Second Isaiah, for whom the term is a standing designation for Israel,[7] it is notoriously difficult to decide whether 'the servant of the Lord' means the prophetic community or a prophetic individual.[8] Both prophet and people owe their existence and loyalty to God as King.[9] Their vocation is to be his servants.

The common calling of people and prophet is further illuminated by the idea that the people, like the prophet, was *owned* by God. Thus, over both God had 'called his name' and this (according to Hebrew idiom[10]) meant that he had claimed them as his own. Jeremiah can say of himself:

I am called by thy name,
O LORD, God of hosts;

and equally of Israel as God's prophetic community:

Yet thou, O LORD, art in the midst of us,
and we are called by thy name;
leave us not.[11]

1. Isa. 41. 8–10.   2. See pp. 51–4.
3. Gen. 26. 24; Exod. 32. 13; Deut. 9. 27; Ezek. 28. 25; Ps. 105. 6.
4. Neh. 1. 10; Pss. 89. 50; 136. 22; Isa. 56. 6; 63. 17; 65. 8–9; 66. 14; cf. Ezek. 37. 25.
5. Num. 12. 7; II Kings 21. 8; Mal. 4. 4; Deut. 34. 5.
6. Jer. 7. 25; 26. 5; 35. 15; 44. 4; Isa. 20. 3; Ezek. 38. 17; Amos 3. 7.
7. Isa. 42. 19; 43. 10; 44. 1–2; 44. 21; 45. 4; 48. 20; 49. 3.
8. Isa. 42. 1–4; 49. 1–6; 50. 4–9; 52. 13–53. 12; see pp. 87ff.
9. Isa. 41. 21; 43. 15; 44. 6.   10. II Sam. 12. 28; Isa. 4. 1.
11. Jer. 15. 16; 14. 9; cf. Isa. 63. 19; 44. 5; Amos 9. 12; Deut. 28. 10.

Like other Old Testament writers, the prophets frequently describe Israel as the Lord's private property – his 'portion' or 'inheritance'[1] and it is an analogous notion which lies behind the familiar affirmation that Israel is the Lord's 'peculiar' people. The Hebrew word often translated 'peculiar' in the English versions means private property when it is used of possessions.[2] Israel was God's personal and private treasure.[3]

The prophets' conception of the relationship between God and Israel as personal is at first sight obscured by the word which dominates the Old Testament writers' presentation of the people's privileged status. This is the word 'covenant'. As it stands, it suggests an impersonal legal contract and, indeed, there was a derivative line of popular thought which identified God's covenant with the law expounding its obligations.[4] There is every probability that the term did, in fact, have its origin in the sphere of law – in the custom of compacts which gave stability to human relationships, when the Hebrews were wandering nomads without any political organization. Thence, it seems, it was borrowed to describe the unique experience of Israel when the disunited tribes were compacted together in a new kind of religious association in the Exodus deliverance.[5] On the whole, the prophets were shy of the term and preferred to describe the relationship between God and Israel in metaphors drawn from marriage and family life.[6] In view of the danger of legalism inherent in the idea of a 'covenant', their reticence is intelligible, but it is important to appreciate that the kind of relationship described by the term in nomadic society was much deeper and more personal than any mere legal contract or commercial bargain. Again and again the emphasis falls on the establishment of a relationship of confidence and peace.[7] One of the most

1. Mic. 7. 14, 18; Jer. 12. 7–8; Isa. 19. 25; 47. 6; Joel 2. 17; 3. 2; cf. Deut. 4. 20; 7. 6; 9. 26.

2. 1 Chron. 29. 3; Eccles. 2. 8.

3. Exod. 19. 5; Deut. 7. 6; 14. 2; 26. 18; Mal. 3. 17; Ps. 135. 4.

4. Deut. 4. 13, 23; 1 Kings 8. 21.   5. Exod. 19. 1–8; 24. 3–8.

6. Hos. 1–3; Jer. 2. 1–3; 3. 1–5; 31; Ezek. 16; Isa. 49. 15; 50. 1; see pp. 56f., 72f., 120.

7. Gen. 21. 27, 32; 26. 26–31; 31. 44; cf. Amos 1. 9.

illuminating of the relationships with which it is associated is that of human friendship. For instance, we read:

> Then Jonathan made a covenant with David, because he loved him as his own soul.[1]

Now the Old Testament has a synonym for human friendship in the word 'peace' (the phrase 'familiar friend' sometimes translates the Hebrew for a 'man of my peace'[2]), and this is the term so often used to describe the complete 'wholesomeness' – the perfect personal harmony – which constituted the inner core of the covenant. The expression 'covenant of peace'[3] is a summary description of God's gracious personal relationship with his people. When Jeremiah had to announce

> I have taken away my peace from this people, says the LORD, my steadfast love and mercy,[4]

he was saying, in effect, that the covenant had been broken by Israel's disloyal rejection of God's friendship.

It is fascinating to discover how each key-word draws us by association still further into the rich personal vocabulary of the great prophets. Thus, Jeremiah's parallel use of 'peace' and 'steadfast love' ('loving-kindness' in the Revised Version) in the verse just quoted[5] introduces us to one of the most profound ideas in Hebrew religion. It is the idea expressed in the word *ḥéṣedh*, here translated 'steadfast love'. Like peace, it is closely connected with the loyalties of friendship. Thus David asks Jonathan to be loyal to the covenant made between them:

> Therefore deal *kindly* (or, keep faith) with your servant, for you have brought your servant into a covenant of the LORD with you.[6]

Later, David recognizes the covenant obligation of *ḥéṣedh* to Jonathan's descendants:

> And David said, 'Is there still any one left of the house of Saul, that I may show him *kindness* for Jonathan's sake?'[7]

1. 1 Sam. 18. 3; cf. 20. 8; Ps. 55. 20.
2. Jer. 20. 10; 38. 22; Obad. 7; Ps. 41. 9.
3. Isa. 54. 10; Ezek. 34. 25; 37. 26; Mal. 2. 5; cf. Num. 25. 12.
4. Jer. 16. 5. 5. Cf. Isa. 54.10.
6. 1 Sam. 20. 8; cf. 18. 1–4; 20. 42. 7. 11 Sam. 9. 1; cf. 9. 3; 16. 17.

The same term is used to describe God's loyalty to his covenant with Israel:

> O LORD, God of Israel, there is no God like thee, in heaven above or on earth beneath, keeping covenant and showing *steadfast love* to thy servants who walk before thee with all their heart;[1]

and equally it describes the personal response to which, by the covenant, Israel is committed:

> I remember the *devotion* of your youth,
>   your love as a bride,
> how you followed me in the wilderness,
>   in a land not sown.[2]

> For I desire *steadfast love* and not sacrifice,
>   the knowledge of God, rather than burnt offerings.[3]

The extraordinary richness of this one term *ḥésedh*, which is an attempt to grasp the inward reality of which 'covenant' is the external expression, eludes all satisfactory translation. The nearest English equivalent is probably 'devotion'. Like the Christian concept of love (*agapé*), it often suggests an un-calculating and steadfast beneficence which is not in the least motivated by the deserts of the recipient.[4] Pre-eminently, it means the devotion of God to Israel,[5] but it also covers the devotion which Israel owes towards God[6] and the 'godly' relationships which ought to exist between fellow-members of the covenant community.[7]

For Hosea (in the last passage we quoted), *ḥésedh*, meaning an attitude towards fellow men which reflected God's love for Israel, was virtually equivalent to what he calls the 'knowledge of God'. This may seem to us a most unexpected association of ideas, but nothing was more natural for an Old Testament writer. Knowledge for the Hebrew was no academic matter of detached intellectual understanding; it meant personal intercourse – experience of that which is known in a way

1. I Kings 8. 23; cf. Deut. 7. 9, 12; II Chron. 6. 14; Neh. 1. 5; 9. 32; Dan. 9. 4.
2. Jer. 2. 2.   3. Hos. 6. 6.   4. Deut. 7. 7–9.
5. Deut. 5. 10; 7. 12; Ps. 103. 17; Jer. 33. 11; Mic. 7. 20.
6. Jer. 2. 2; Hos. 6. 4.
7. Hos. 6. 6; Mic. 6. 6–8; see, further, pp. 104–10, 118f.

which affects the knower.[1] Knowledge, thus understood, made its impact on the will as well as the mind and issued in personal concern and active response. To know God was equivalent to recognizing his works and accepting his personal demands.[2] Ignorance of God was shown in a lack of concern.[3] When we appreciate that 'knowledge' in Hebrew thought connotes personal concern, it is not surprising that the experience of being known by God has a place (like the other concepts we have briefly touched on) in the prophets' presentation both of their own intimate vocation and of their convictions about the prophetic mission of the people. There is a world of difference between 'having a religion' and being found and known by God. Thus Jeremiah can speak of himself as one known of God:

> Before I formed you in the womb I *knew* you,
> and before you were born I consecrated you;

> But thou, O LORD, *knowest* me;
> thou seest me, and triest my mind toward thee.[4]

And Amos and Hosea can sum up the covenant relationship between God and Israel in terms of God's 'knowledge', that is, his personal concern for his people:

> You only have I *known*
> of all the families of the earth;

> It was I who *knew* you in the wilderness,
> in the land of drought.[5]

A living personal relationship – like a human friendship – develops so intimate a quality that no account of its historical origin can adequately expound its full meaning. This may well account for the interesting fact that the prophets are content with the most general references to the actual *events*

1. Thus, one can 'know' quietness (Job. 20. 20), sickness (Isa. 53. 3), the loss of children (Isa. 47. 8), and divine punishment (Ezek. 25. 14); cf. Gen. 4. 1; 1 Kings 1. 4.
2. Jer. 22. 16; see, further, pp. 115–23.
3. Hos. 4. 1, 6; 5. 4; Isa. 1. 3; 5. 13; Jer. 10. 25.
4. Jer. 1. 5; 12. 3; cf. Deut. 34. 10.
5. Amos 3. 2; Hos. 13. 5; cf. 5. 3; Nahum 1. 7.

of the Exodus from Egypt. They never appear to isolate this one historical occurrence. Rather, they set it alongside subsequent and present experience which convinced them of God's abiding love for his people.[1] Sometimes, they even go so far as to say in effect: 'Stop thinking about what God has done for you in the past and be more ready to respond to his grace in the present.' This is a salutary reminder of the continuing care of the *living* God which every reader of the Bible needs more often than he may suppose. The Biblical revelation always stands in danger of becoming a curious fossil, not 'rooted' so much as buried in history. Popular religion, which has lost touch with the prophets' sense of the present, shows an incurable tendency to waste its energy in expanding its tradition backwards to a remote, assured, but irrelevant past, rather than forwards to grapple with the spiritual problems – the exile – of our present world. For all his emphasis on the importance of the Exodus, Second Isaiah was a true prophet when he called upon Israel to turn from memory to lively expectation, from the past to the present and the future:

> Remember not the former things,
>   nor consider the things of old.
> Behold, I am doing a new thing;
>   now it springs forth, do you not perceive it?[2]

The elaboration of the patriarchal narratives marks a decline from this vital prophetic awareness and it is in this sense that they represent a more popular type of religion. Nevertheless, the stories in Genesis have considerable value if we read them as a commentary on the central prophetic tradition of Israel's vocation. Although they are couched in historical terms, what they really attempt to convey is not so much an alternative history of Israel's origin, as an assessment of the profound religious meaning of the covenant relationship inaugurated by Moses. The Hebrews wrote 'history', when we should write philosophy. Whereas we might say that in delivering the tribesmen from Egypt, God disclosed his 'eternal' love for Israel, the Hebrew most naturally said that the God

---

1. Amos 2. 10–11; Hos. 12. 13.
2. Isa. 43. 18–19; cf. Jer. 16. 14–15; Mic. 7. 15.

of Moses was 'the God of Abraham, the God of Isaac, and the God of Jacob'.[1]

PERILS AND AFFIRMATIONS

The new and untempered faith of the people of the Exodus was exposed to formidable temptations when they established themselves in Palestine. A religion born in the desert was entirely strange to the diehard pagan culture of the agricultural society of Canaan and quite unaccustomed to the political machinations to which the two kingdoms of Israel and Judah were always relentlessly exposed. At the risk of oversimplifying the infinitely complex situation which resulted from this mingling of the old culture with the new faith, we may select five of the great perils which the prophets had to face and notice the positive affirmations by which they maintained and enriched the Mosaic tradition. From the struggle in which they engaged, there emerged a deep and mature conception of Israel's vocation. The nature of the covenant was revealed in conflict.

Amos affirms the moral nature of Israel's vocation

The prophet Amos had to fight a type of complacent self-assurance which appealed to the privileges of Israel's vocation and ignored all its responsibilities. His contemporaries had arrogantly nationalized God and taken him over as one of their assets. In many ways, the religious jingoism of the Israelites in the eighth century B.C. is akin to the ancient tribal religion of the Semitic world, which was based on the idea that each group had its own special god. It is possible that the book of Genesis illustrates this conception of private deities, when it records the names of the gods of the patriarchs – the 'Shield of Abraham', the 'Kinsman of Isaac' and the 'Champion of Jacob'.[2] The name of Isaac's god further illustrates how the relationship between a god and his group was conceived of in the most intimate terms. The god was a member of the family

1. Exod. 3. 6.　　　　2. Gen. 15. 1; 31. 42, 53; 49. 24.

and shared with his children a common blood. Thus, for example, when the devotees of Chemosh, the god of the Moab-
ites, were called the 'sons' and 'daughters' of Chemosh,[1]
much more than a picturesque metaphor was being used. We
may well imagine that such 'homely' religion was in the
worst sense smug. The god with whom it was concerned was
as weak in his impact on the 'family' of his worshippers as the
most indulgent of human fathers. His 'will' (if, indeed, he
could be thought to have had a mind of his own) was little
more than a reflection of current social practice; there was no
question of its being a disturbing or determinative factor. The
one asset with which he appears to have been credited was
the power to promote his children's welfare. It was believed
that Father had influence in the world of affairs; he was
worth coaxing on occasion.

Now the people of northern Israel to whom Amos addressed
his message in the middle of the eighth century B.C. had fallen
into the habit of thinking of God in some such terms as these.
They needed no persuading that he was intimately concerned
with their interests, for they were eagerly and confidently looking forward to the day when he would take some sort of decisive action and make them the prosperous overlords of the
inhabited world. They called this day the Day of the Lord,
but, in fact, they thought of it as a gala-day for themselves.
With withering irony, Amos assured the Israelites that the
Day of the Lord would come, as they said, but not with the
result they expected. It was the day of the *Lord*, when he
would take action in a way truly characteristic of his nature,
and as that was essentially *moral righteousness*, it would bring
judgement upon Israel. For the people to invite it, was to invite disaster:

> Woe to you who desire the day of the LORD!
>> Why would you have the day of the LORD?
> It is darkness, and not light.[2]

It was true that Israel had been called to enjoy a particularly intimate relationship with God.[3] It had been forgotten,

1. Num. 21. 29; Jer. 48. 46.
2. Amos 5. 18; cf. Isa. 2. 12–17; Zeph. 1. 14–16; Joel 1. 15; 2. 1, 11, 31;
3. 14; see, further, pp. 147ff.   3. Amos 3. 2; 2. 9–12.

however, that God was not a national convenience like the gods of the heathen, but a God of absolute righteousness. Israel's privileged intimacy with God, therefore, made the people's moral corruption all the more intolerable.[1] Unless there was a radical reformation (and, for the most part, this seemed to Amos too much to hope for), the Day of the Lord would coincide with the dispersal of the chosen people into 'exile beyond Damascus' – the slaves of the ruthless Assyrians.[2] Their judgement would be God's self-disclosure.

The covenant between God and Israel was not an indissoluble natural relationship, nor was its stability assured for all time by the deliverance of the people from Egypt. In a surprising declaration, Amos undermined the self-confidence which the conventional appeal to the Exodus seemed to justify:

'Are you not like the Ethiopians to me,
  O people of Israel?' says the LORD.
'Did I not bring up Israel from the land of Egypt,
  and the Philistines from Caphtor
    and the Syrians from Kir?
Behold, the eyes of the Lord GOD are upon
.   the sinful kingdom,
  and I will destroy it from the surface of the ground ...'[3]

God, the righteous sovereign of all the nations of the world,[4] had directed the migrations of the hated Philistines and the Syrians against whom Israel had had so often to defend herself. Israel's Exodus, therefore, endowed her with no immunity from judgement. Her vocation was conditional upon her moral and spiritual fidelity to God who had called her. Unless in the people's life 'justice rolled down like waters, and righteousness like an everflowing stream',[5] the covenant would be dissolved and Israel's privileged status would become an empty theory.

1. On the rottenness of Israel's social and economic life, see pp. 105–10.
2. Amos 5. 27. There is a ray of hope in 5. 15 and 7. 1–6, but the prophet's later message is that Israel will be destroyed (7. 7–9; 8. 1–3; 9. 1–4).
3. Amos 9. 7–8; cf. 5. 14 ('as you have said'); 9. 10; Mic. 3. 11; Deut. 29. 19.
4. Amos 1. 3–2. 3; see, further, pp. 117, 119f.
5. Amos 5. 24. On the meaning of 'righteousness', see pp. 115–19.

Hosea affirms the personal nature of Israel's vocation

Religion must not be, indeed in the last analysis cannot be, divorced from everyday life. From the moment the desert fathers settled in Palestine, it was clear that they must come to terms with the complex agricultural life of its inhabitants. This necessity, however, was fraught with danger and difficulty. The God of Israel had disclosed himself not in nature but in action; the sphere of his operations was ongoing history and not the recurrent cycle of the seasons. On arrival in Palestine, the Israelites discovered that the needs of the farmer were thoroughly provided for by fertility cults, which flourished 'upon every high hill and under every green tree'. With the evidence of the temple library of Ras Shamra on the north coast of Syria before us, it is now clear that these cults were part of one of the most sophisticated religious systems of the ancient world. The 'baalim' of the Old Testament are now seen to be local varieties of the great god Baal, chief of the many deities which swarm through the mythology of Canaanite religion.[1] The sordid and revolting rites of the village sanctuaries in Palestine were (by and large) a provincial version of the elaborate liturgies and the developed system of sacred prostitution over which the hereditary High Priest presided in his sumptuous temple at Ras Shamra. It requires little imagination to appreciate that the Israelites were sorely tempted to abandon their God for Baal and, being now in Canaan, to do as the Canaanites did. The sympathetic magic of Canaanite religion was believed to harness the fertility of nature upon which their new agricultural life depended; it was firmly entrenched in the sanctuaries they took over as they conquered the land; in every sense, it seemed unavoidable.[2] Israel did not know, as Hosea pointed out, that it was their God, who 'gave her the grain, the wine, and the oil'.[3] In consequence, the worship of the God of the Exodus was often retained in little more than name; sometimes, even nominal allegiance was abandoned in favour of Baal.

1. Hos. 2. 17; 11. 2; 13. 1; 1 Kings 18. 21; Jer. 2. 8, 23; 7. 9; 9. 14.
2. Deut. 12. 29–30; Hos. 7. 14–16.
3. Hos. 2. 8. For similar extension of God's activity in the sphere of nature, see Deut. 33. 13–17; 1 Kings 18–19.

It was Hosea, a contemporary of Amos and himself a man of the northern kingdom, who of all the great prophets was most revolted by the Canaanite practices of his fellow-countrymen. They seemed to him to demonstrate and ingrain more deeply Israel's decline from the faith of the desert. Worst of all, they betrayed the people's fundamental insensitiveness to God's love. They were totally unaware of that loyal response which the covenant demanded. The experience of his unhappy marriage with Gomer – and, through this tragic situation, of a love which even her unfaithfulness was unable to quench – had taught Hosea that the essential characteristic of the relationship between God and Israel was its personal quality.[1]

It is not surprising, therefore, that his oracles, more than those of any other prophet, denounce the Israelites' magical rites and clutter of religious paraphernalia – their appointed feasts and superstitious sacrifices, their images, fertility symbols and apparatus for divination.[2] All these represented to Hosea, his countrymen's *horrible*[3] ingratitude – an ingratitude so base as to deserve the name adultery.[4] Lewdness had answered love. God's people – like the prophet's wife Gomer – had abandoned the charitable devotion of her divine 'husband' for the sensual tyranny of a Canaanite 'lord'.[5]

It is with such telling personal metaphors that Hosea (like his spiritual son, Jeremiah, in the next century[6]) characterizes the breach of the covenant made between God and Israel in the ideal honeymoon period of the wilderness – 'in the days of her youth ... when she came up from the land of Egypt'. Israel had now forgotten her Maker, wilfully rejected knowledge of God,[7] and deserved to perish.[8] Hosea, however, did not draw the remorseless conclusion of Amos. He asserted

1. Hos. 1–3; cf. 11. 1–2.
2. Hos. 2. 13; 3. 4; 4. 13–14; 7. 14; 8. 13; 9. 6; 13. 1–3.
3. Hos. 6. 10; cf. Jer. 5. 30; 18. 13; 23. 14.
4. Hos. 4. 12; 9. 1; cf. Jer. 13. 27.
5. Hos. 2. 16.
6. Jer. 2. 2–3; 3. 19–20; 31. 9, 20, 32.
7. Hos. 8. 14; 4. 1, 6; 5. 4; 6. 6; see, further, pp. 65f.
8. Hos. 1. 9; 5. 6, 12, 14–15; 9. 3, 15; 13. 7–10.

that the power of God would be found in his *pathos* and his superiority to man in the grace of forgiveness:

> How can I give you up, O Ephraim!
>> How can I hand you over, O Israel!
> How can I make you like Admah!
>> How can I treat you like Zeboiim![1]
> My heart recoils within me,
>> my compassion grows warm and tender.
> I will not execute my fierce anger,
>> I will not again destroy Ephraim;
> *For I am God and not man* ...[2]

Again, the prophet had dared to draw on his own personal experience. He ascribed to God the anguish of a rejected lover and represented him as courting the people back to their original intimacy:

> Therefore, behold, I will allure her,
>> and bring her into the wilderness,
>> and speak tenderly to her.[3]

And I will betroth you to me for ever; I will betroth you to me in righteousness and in justice, in steadfast love, and in mercy. I will betroth you to me in faithfulness; and you shall know the LORD.[4]

You shall know the Lord. For Hosea, this was the end and the means of Israel's vocation as the People of God. If the mechanical and immoral observances of Canaan are to be called 'religion', another word altogether will have to be found for this prophetic conception of personal intercourse with God. It was new even in Hebrew religion, and although it has been immeasurably enriched by Christian devotion, it has never been superseded.

Isaiah affirms the transcendent *nature of Israel's vocation*

Not all the perils which the prophets diagnosed in Israel's national life sprang from the soil of Palestine. A glance at a map of the ancient world reminds one how Israel's territory occupied a central and exposed position in a crescent-shaped

1. Admah and Zeboiim were cities of the plain which were utterly destroyed with Sodom and Gomorrah: Deut. 29. 23; Jer. 49. 18.
2. Hos. 11. 8–9.　　　3. Hos. 2. 14.　　　4. Hos. 2. 19–20.

strip of fertile land. This 'fertile crescent' stretched from the Persian Gulf in the east with Babylon at its tip, up through the valleys of the Tigris and Euphrates to Assyria, across to Damascus (an important and prosperous trading centre), and then down along the coast-land of Palestine. It ended with Egypt and the valley of the Nile as its western and most southerly point. Israel's home, therefore, was at once a commercial bridge and a military no-man's-land between the rival civilizations of Egypt and Mesopotamia.

Commercial and political ambitions have always been potential enemies to spiritual integrity and it is clear that Israel caught the infection of both from her more civilized neighbours. She was, of course, never really strong enough for independent action and so she sought trade and military alliances with the great powers on her borders. As part of the same policy, her kings took foreign queens and with them came their gods. When, for instance, Solomon tried to cement the disintegrating fabric of his kingdom by promiscuous marriage, his court admitted a whole spate of foreign cults.[1] When Ahab took the disastrous Jezebel to wife in order to win the support of Tyre, the worship of the Phoenician Baal received royal patronage.[2] Again, the almost complete annihilation of the Israelite faith in the reign of Manasseh two centuries later was a direct consequence of the king's subservience to Assyria – just as the religious reformation undertaken by Josiah, his successor, was possible only because Assyria at that time was too weak to intervene.[3]

But such religious syncretism was but one of the many symptoms of a deeper disorder in Israel's national life. The adoption of many gods betrayed, as the prophets were quick to point out, a radical lack of faith in the sufficiency of the Lord. This was clearly demonstrated by the political factions in the nation, which were always intriguing for foreign alliances. When Hosea, for example, insisted that

> Ephraim is like a dove,
>> silly and without sense,
>>> calling to Egypt, going to Assyria,[4]

1. I Kings 11. 1–8.   2. I Kings 16. 30–3; see pp. 41–4, 71.
3. II Kings 21–3.   4. Hos. 7. 11; cf. 7. 8–9; 8. 8–10.

he did not mean that Egyptian and Assyrian religion had found their way into Israel. He meant that Israel herself had lost her way. She had mistaken her religious vocation for a political destiny – 'like all the nations.'[1] Her kings, for example, had arrogantly claimed an authority which ran counter to the sovereignty which God had delegated to them. The prophetic diagnosis of Israel's political disease is reflected in the many Old Testament passages which express a profound distrust of the monarchy.[2]

The protests of the prophets against the distortion of Israel's vocation by political ambitions and entanglements will best be understood from the oracles of Isaiah, the son of Amoz, who prophesied in Jerusalem during the second half of the eighth century B.C. It was during this period that Assyria overran and re-colonized the northern kingdom (in 721 B.C.) and reduced the southern kingdom to little more than the city of Jerusalem (in 701 B.C.). The background of Isaiah's ministry, therefore, was a constant series of intrigues among the small states of Palestine to form alliances against the Assyrian menace. The most notable of these was that led by Pekah of the northern kingdom and Rezin of Damascus in 734 B.C.[3] The ambition of these two kings was to win the support of Judah against Assyria. When Ahaz, the Judean king, proved unco-operative, this 'Syro-Ephraimitic coalition' (as it is called) threatened Jerusalem. The book of Isaiah contains a vivid account of a famous meeting which took place between the prophet and the king, when Ahaz was inspecting the defences of the besieged city.[4] In abject terror, Ahaz was on the point of appealing to Assyria for help. Isaiah's demand on this occasion for a steadfast faith epitomizes his greatest single contribution to the distinctive religion of Israel:

Take heed, be quiet, do not fear, and do not let your heart be faint because of these two smouldering stumps of firebrands, at the

1. 1 Sam. 8. 5; Deut. 17. 14.
2. Hos. 7. 3–7; 8. 4; 9. 9 (Gibeah being the home of Saul, Israel's first king: 1 Sam. 10. 26); 9. 15 (Gilgal being the place where Saul was acclaimed king: 1 Sam. 11. 15); 10. 3, 9; 13. 10–11; cf. Judg. 8. 23; 1 Sam. 10. 17–24; Deut. 17. 14–20.
3. II Kings 16.　　　　　4. Isa. 7. 1–9.

fierce anger of Rezin and Syria and the son of Remaliah.[1]

> If you will not believe,
> surely you shall not be established.[2]

Only if Ahaz stood *firm* in God's sufficiency, would he be *confirmed* in his political independence – the pun in the Hebrew for 'believe' and 'established' cannot adequately be represented in English. Isaiah assured the king that the threat from the northern coalition would be short-lived, that it would, in fact, disappear within two or three years. This is the point of the famous 'Immanuel' prophecy. Before a young woman known to the king could marry and see her first child outgrow the baby-stage, the danger would have passed. Therefore, the boy could be named Immanuel, meaning 'God is with us'.[3] Ahaz ignored Isaiah's assurance and appealed to Assyria.

However we assess the prophet's political sagacity, the true significance of his attitude is to be found in the conviction that God's guardianship of his people was more than equal to all political contingencies. If Israel remained faithful to her calling, she was stronger than these damp squibs in the north and had nothing to fear from the biggest battalions the nations could muster. Throughout the troubled period of his ministry, Isaiah consistently demanded quiet confidence and faith and, in consequence, the refusal of all political entanglements. Those who intrigued with Egypt – a country which had always played the part of the snake-in-the-grass in Palestinian affairs – are frequently denounced in no uncertain terms:

> Woe to those who go down to Egypt for help
> and rely on horses,
> who trust in chariots because they are many
> and in horsemen because they are very strong,
> but do not look to the Holy One of Israel
> or consult the LORD![4]

Isaiah tried to teach Israel that she was not called to the dizzy

1. Isa. 7. 4; the 'son of Remaliah' is Pekah, king of Israel.
2. Isa. 7. 9.　　　　3. Isa. 7. 10–17.
4. Isa. 31. 1; cf. 18. 1–7; 22. 15–25; 28. 14–22; 29. 15–16; 30. 1–7.

and precarious heights of imperial prestige, but rather to a spiritual and moral service of God – in a serenity like his own:

> For thus the LORD said to me:
> 'I will quietly look from my dwelling
>   like clear heat in sunshine,
>   like a cloud of dew in the heat of harvest.'[1]

> For thus said the Lord GOD, the Holy One of Israel,
> 'In returning and rest you shall be saved;
>   in quietness and in trust shall be your strength.'[2]

From first to last, Isaiah's oracles convey an indelible impression of a single-minded man of God standing calm and imperturbable as the conflicts of the world eddy powerlessly about his feet. He upheld the moral and personal conception of Israel's mission which we found in Amos and Hosea, but he gave it stature and a larger perspective by his simple and profound confidence in God at a time when the whole political pattern in Palestine was being shattered by Assyria. He held firm to his faith through the troubled history of his age by interpreting it in the light of his initial vision of God. Israel, like the prophet, had been called by the King whose glory filled the whole earth.[3] Small wonder that her mission transcended the political intrigues of one small corner of it.

His disciples and interpreters, it would seem, have not been content to leave the matter there. They have tried to gild the lily by ascribing to the prophet an explicit promise that God would protect Jerusalem against all the assaults of the enemy:

Therefore thus says the LORD concerning the king of Assyria: He shall not come into this city, or shoot an arrow there, or come before it with a shield, or cast up a siege-mound against it. By the way that he came, by the same he shall return, and he shall not come into this city, says the LORD. For I will defend this city to save it, for my own sake and for the sake of my servant David.[4]

Isaiah's close connexion with the court and royal family makes it unsafe to deny the possibility that the divine protection of Jerusalem had a place in his teaching,[5] but it is worth

1. Isa. 18. 4.   2. Isa. 30. 15; cf. 28. 16.
3. Isa. 6. 3.   4. Isa. 37. 33–5.
5. Isa. 29. 7–8; 30. 30–1; 31. 5; see, further, p. 158.

77

noticing that at least on one occasion he denounced the jubila-
tion of its citizens when – physically – the capital was spared:

> What do you mean that you have gone up,
>   all of you, to the housetops,
> you who are full of shoutings,
>   tumultuous city, exultant town?
> Your slain are not slain with the sword
>   or dead in battle ...
> In that day the Lord GOD of hosts,
>   called to weeping and mourning,
>   to baldness and girding with sackcloth;
> and behold, joy and gladness ...[1]

Flushed with political victory, the people had missed its
spiritual meaning: 'But you did not look to him who did it, or
have regard for him who planned it long ago.'[2] If, therefore,
we ascribe to the prophet (and not only to his disciples) a
belief in the inviolability of Jerusalem, we ought to be clear
that what he was concerned to uphold was the inviolability
of God's purpose in history:

> The LORD of hosts has sworn:
> 'As I have planned,
>   so shall it be,
> and as I have purposed,
>   so shall it stand,
> that I will break the Assyrian in my land,
>   and upon my mountains trample him under foot;
> and his yoke shall depart from them,
>   and his burden from their shoulder.'
> This is the purpose that is purposed
>   concerning the whole earth;
> and this is the hand that is stretched out
>   over all the nations.
> For the LORD of hosts has purposed,
>   and who will annul it?
> His hand is stretched out,
>   and who will turn it back?[3]

Israel's vocation was to bear witness amid the relativities of

---

1. Isa. 22. 1–2, 12–13.   2. Isa. 22. 11.
3. Isa. 14. 24–7; cf. 10. 5–16; 37. 22–9.

history to that transcendent purpose by which ultimately it is governed.

Jeremiah affirms the inward *nature of Israel's vocation*

Jeremiah is the prophet of life through death. During his forty years' ministry (626–586 B.C.), he witnessed the political disintegration of his country and shared its final collapse. So far from regretting the disappearance of Judah's national sovereignty, he consistently urged that the Babylonian invader should not be resisted.[1] He had searched diligently for something in Israel's life which was worth preserving, but had found absolutely nothing:

> An appalling and horrible thing
>   has happened in the land:
> the prophets prophesy falsely,
>   and the priests rule at their direction;
> my people love to have it so,
>   but what will you do when the end comes?[2]

What Jeremiah saw in Jerusalem shook him to the very foundations of his being. The universe, it seemed, was being reduced to the primeval chaos from which God had originally redeemed it:

> I looked on the earth, and lo, it was waste and void;
>   and to the heavens, and they had no light.
> I looked on the mountains, and lo, they were quaking,
>   and all the hills moved to and fro.
> I looked, and lo, there was no man,
>   and all the birds of the air had fled.
> I looked, and lo, the fruitful land was a desert,
>   and all its cities were laid in ruins
>   before the LORD, before his fierce anger.[3]

A generation like our own, which has lived through – and 'seen through' – so much, ought to be able to appreciate some-

1. Jer. 21. 8–10; 37. 10, 13–14; 38. 17–18.
2. Jer. 5. 30–1; cf. 2. 1–37; 3. 1–5, 19–20; 5. 1–14, 26–9; 6. 9–15; 7. 16–20; 9. 2–9.
3. Jer. 4. 23–6; cf. Gen. 1. 2.

thing of the depths of Jeremiah's despair. Wherever he turned, he encountered 'nothingness':

> What wrong did your fathers find in me
>   that they went far from me,
> and went after worthlessness, and became worthless?
>
> Has a nation changed its gods,
>   even though they are no gods?
> But my people have changed their glory
>   for that which does not profit.
> Be appalled, O heavens, at this,
>   be shocked, be utterly desolate,
>   says the LORD,
>   or my people have committed two evils:
>   they have forsaken me,
> the fountain of living waters,
>   and hewed out cisterns for themselves,
> broken cisterns,
>   that can hold no water.[1]

It would be a mistake to suppose that Jeremiah's diagnosis of Israel's apostasy from 'the fountain of living waters' was simply her drift from orthodox worship to the cults of Baal. Orthodoxy itself was included in the condemnation. The prophet had sacrificed the comfort afforded by traditional religion and wandered in a lonely spiritual wilderness of doubt and despair. Like Job, he had explored the naked reality of man's predicament. Out of his physical suffering and intense mental anguish,[2] there had been born an unmediated awareness of God to which 'religion' was utterly irrelevant. At the crisis of his ministry, Jeremiah went to the Temple, declared war on all that it stood for, and prophesied its destruction.[3] Religion must die, he had come to believe, to make way for the living God. That was his uncompromising conviction. The Israelite tradition had always been uneasy about the possibility of falling into the pagan conception of the

1. Jer. 2. 5, 11–13.
2. Jer. 4. 19–22; 10. 23–5; 11. 18–23; 12. 1–6; 15. 10–21; 17. 14–18; 18. 18–23; 20. 7–18.
3. Jer. 7. 1–15; 26. 1–6; cf. 12. 7; Mic. 3. 12.

Temple as the 'house' where God dwelt,[1] and in the remarkable prayer of Solomon at the dedication of the Temple, the whole idea of localizing God is explicitly rejected:

> But will God indeed dwell on the earth? Behold, heaven and the highest heaven cannot contain thee; how much less this house which I have built![2]

Although care was taken to describe the Temple as the place where God had 'tabernacled his *name*'[3] (thus avoiding the suggestion that it was his dwelling in any ordinary sense), Jeremiah saw clearly that it had become a fetish: 'Do not trust', he warned, 'in these deceptive words: "This is the temple of the LORD, the temple of the LORD, the temple of the LORD."'[4] If this magical incantation exposed the false assurance engendered by 'religion', so also did the whole familiar system of sacrificial worship.[5] That Jeremiah intended an unqualified repudiation of sacrifice is clear from the remorseless consistency with which he discards every external substitute for that dynamic and inward intercourse with God which he had discovered in his agonizing spiritual struggle. The ark of the covenant, for example, must be forgotten[6] and the book-wisdom of the scribes is dismissed as being no true knowledge of God.[7] Like St Paul later, he denied the importance of ritual circumcision and demanded a circumcision of the *heart* – 'for he is not a real Jew who is one outwardly, nor is true circumcision something external and physical. He is a Jew who is one inwardly, and real circumcision is a matter of the heart, spiritual and not literal.'[8]

He is a Jew who is one inwardly. This expresses the core of Jeremiah's conviction and it explains why the Judeans who were exiled to Babylon in 597 B.C. were regarded by the prophet as fortunate in leaving Jerusalem; they had lost nothing but the hindrance of 'religion':

1. Solomon's temple was called the 'house of the Lord'; I Kings 6. 1.
2. I Kings 8. 27; cf. II Sam. 7. 4–6.   3. Deut. 12. 5, 11.
4. Jer. 7. 4.
5. Jer. 7. 21–8; cf. 6. 20; 11. 15; see, further, pp. 109–14.
6. Jer. 3. 16.   7. Jer. 8. 8–13.
8. Romans 2. 28–9; Jer. 4. 4; 9. 26.

But seek the welfare of the city where I have sent you into exile, and pray to the LORD on its behalf, for in its welfare you will find your welfare.[1]

There could not possibly be any clearer break with the notion that God was a 'landlord', localized like the gods of the nations in his own special area and served through his own special cult.[2]

The inwardness of the relationship between God and man, which Jeremiah had discovered in lonely spiritual travail, is given complete and consummate expression in his oracle on the New Covenant:

Behold, the days are coming, says the LORD, when I will make a new covenant with the house of Israel and the house of Judah, not like the covenant which I made with their fathers when I took them by the hand to bring them out of the land of Egypt, my covenant which they broke, though I was their husband, says the LORD. But this is the covenant which I will make with the house of Israel after those days, says the LORD: I will put my law within them, and I will write it upon their hearts; and I will be their God, and they shall be my people. And no longer shall each man teach his neighbour and each his brother, saying, 'Know the LORD,' for they shall all know me, from the least of them to the greatest, says the LORD; for I will forgive their iniquity, and I will remember their sin no more.[3]

Just how extraordinarily new this conception of the covenant is, and how greatly it differed from the religion which it replaced, may be judged from the way in which it is used by the writer of the Epistle to the Hebrews to characterize the new covenant inaugurated by Christ, as contrasted with the obsolete covenant of Judaism.[4] Although Jeremiah still thinks of Israel as the Chosen People with whom God will enter into the new relationship, its intimate nature was clearly a step on the road towards an explicit recognition of its universality. Israel had now become, at least in vision if not yet in ıact, the community of all who sincerely sought and found the Lord.

1. Jer. 29. 7; cf. 24. 1–10.
2. Cf. 1 Sam. 26. 19; II Kings 5. 17; 17. 24–8; 1 Kings 20. 23.
3. Jer. 31. 31–4.
4. Hebrews 8. 8–13; 10. 15–17; cf. echoes in II Corinthians 3. 6; 1 Corinthians 11. 25; Luke 22. 20; Matthew 26. 28.

Second Isaiah affirms the ultimate *nature of Israel's vocation*

After the fall of Jerusalem in 586 B.C., Nebuchadrezzar deported to Babylon the cream of Judah's manhood. Once in exile, many of the Jews settled down among the Babylonians as Jeremiah had advised them to do.[1] Others kept themselves separate from the society of their conquerors and prepared for their return to their own land. These were the people who determined the form of post-exilic Judaism and to a very large extent the final shape of the Old Testament. Between these two groups, the settlers and the separatists, there must have been a great number of Jews who were simply bewildered:

> Why do you say, O Jacob,
>   and speak, O Israel,
> 'My way is hid from the LORD,
>   and my right is disregarded by my God'?[2]

It was to such men that the anonymous prophet of the exile addressed the oracles we have received as Chapters 40–55 of the book of Isaiah.

The peril of disillusionment, which threatened every national religion when it came up against adverse political fortune, was the problem which had to be faced after the shock of the deportation to Babylon. Like the women who told Jeremiah that they were reverting to the worship of the Queen of Heaven, because the prophetic faith of Israel had failed to provide what they wanted,[3] many of the exiles must previously have thought of their religious practice as an insurance policy against national disaster.[4] They too had been disillusioned. The policy did not cover 'acts of God'. There is little wonder that the national religions of Moab, Ammon, and the rest fizzled out when they failed to pass this exacting test. As the gods of the nations, it would appear, were scarcely more than personifications of social welfare and national independence, they were inevitably discarded when their territories were absorbed into the great empires on their borders. The

1. Jer. 29. 5–7, 27–8; cf. Neh. 1. 11; 2. 1–8; Ezra 2. 68–9; Ezek. 8. 1; 14. 1; 20. 1; 24. 18.
2. Isa. 40. 27; cf. 42. 22–4; 49. 14; see, further, pp. 138ff.
3. Jer. 44. 18.   4. Jer. 7. 9–10.

God of Israel was not forgotten in this way, because he continued to confront his people with judgement and mercy, trhough the events of history as interpreted by his servants the prophets.

Second Isaiah, prophet and poet, delivered his oracles at one of the most critical periods in the history not only of Israel but of the whole Near East, when the era of the great Semitic empires was drawing to its close. Already the armies of Cyrus [1] were victoriously extending the bounds of the Persian Empire, and the collapse of Babylon, where the Jews were locked in exile, was imminent. Second Isaiah rises to this tremendous occasion and with incomparable vision expounds the expected deliverance in the total context of God's purpose for Israel and, through Israel, for the world. No historical scene has ever been given so luminous a frame.

The coming return of the exiles to Palestine [2] and the restoration of Jerusalem [3] are nothing less, the prophet proclaims, than the first events of that New Age which represents the climax of God's purpose. He is about to disclose himself as the Redeemer of Israel [4] in a second and more marvellous Exodus from bondage. [5]

In studying the poems of Second Isaiah, it is tempting to concentrate exclusively on the magnificent passages which present his vision of God's universal sovereignty, and then draw a straight contrast between this allegedly 'broadminded' outlook and the 'narrow nationalism' which appears in the writings of the post-exilic age – Haggai, Zechariah, Nehemiah, and Ezra. [6] Such a simple universalist message, however, would hardly have raised the drooping spirits of the exiles and that, we must remember, was the prophet's immediate task. In any case, such an emphasis cannot survive a fair examination of the literary evidence. Second Isaiah is, in fact, more passionately concerned with the unique privilege

1. Isa. 44. 28; 45. 1.
2. Isa. 40. 9–10; 43. 20–1; 49. 9–11; 51. 11; 55. 12–13.
3. Isa. 44. 26; 45. 13; 49. 16–17; 51. 3; 52. 1, 9; 54. 11–14.
4. Isa. 41. 14; 43. 14; 44. 6, 24; 47. 4; 48. 17; 49. 7, 26; 54. 5, 8.
5. Isa. 43. 5–7, 19–12; 45. 13; 48. 20–1; 49. 9–11; 52. 2; 55. 12–13.
6. Hag. 2. 10–14; Zech. 1. 18–21; 12. 1–13. 6; 14. 1–21; Neh. 13. 1–3, 23–31; Ezra 4. 1–5; 10. 10–12; see, further, pp. 152–7.

of Israel than any of his predecessors.[1] It is not for nothing that he borrows from Isaiah of Jerusalem the 'Holy One *of Israel*' as a title for God.[2]

We can appreciate the full force of Second Isaiah's sense of Israel's vocation only if we first recognize the magnificence of his conception of God's *absolute sovereignty*. It often finds expression in direct statement:

> Thus says the LORD, the King of Israel
> and his Redeemer, the LORD of hosts:
> 'I am the first and I am the last;
> besides me there is no god.
> Who is like me? Let him proclaim it,
> let him declare and set it forth before me.
> Who has announced from of old the things to come?
> Let them tell us what is yet to be.
> Fear not, nor be afraid;
> have I not told you from of old and declared it?
> And you are my witnesses!
> Is there a God besides me?
> There is no Rock; I know not any.'[3]

It is also reflected in the prophet's presentation of Israel's Redeemer as the Creator and Sustainer of the whole universe[4] and, again, in the pitiless irony with which he exposes the futility of the idols which the Babylonians ignorantly worshipped.[5] If we drain off the life from the prophet's poetry and compress the residue into a formal doctrine of 'monotheism', we shall miss the whole point of these superb chapters. Second Isaiah was not concerned to establish the belief that there was only one God (that, with his predecessors, he took for granted). What he was concerned to do was to convince the despondent exiles that it was *their* God, who had 'measured the waters in the hollow of his hand ... and weighed the mountains in scales', that it was *their* God, the Holy One of Israel, whose purpose governed all things from the Creation of the world to the coming of Cyrus:

1. Isa. 41. 8–10; 42. 1; 43. 10, 20; 44. 1–2; 45. 4; 49. 7.
2. Isa. 41. 14, 16, 20; 43. 3; 49. 7.
3. Isa. 44. 6–8; 45. 5, 6, 21; cf. 41. 4; 43. 15; 46. 4; 48. 12.
4. Isa. 40. 15, 17, 23–4; 42. 5; 43. 1–7; 54. 16–17.
5. Isa. 40. 18–20; 44. 9–20; 45. 20; 46. 1–2; cf. 41. 24, 29.

Thus says the LORD, your Redeemer,
>who formed you from the womb:
'I am the LORD, who made all things,
>who stretched out the heavens alone,
>who spread out the earth – Who was with me? –
who frustrates the omens of liars,
>and makes fools of diviners;
who turns wise men back,
>and makes their knowledge foolish;
who confirms the word of his servant,
>and performs the counsel of his messengers;
who says of Jerusalem, "She shall be inhabited,"
>and of the cities of Judah, "They shall be built,
>and I will raise up their ruins;"
who says to the deep, "Be dry,
>I will dry up your rivers;"
who says of Cyrus, "He is my shepherd,
>and he shall fulfil all my purpose;"
saying of Jerusalem, "She shall be built,"
>and of the temple, "Your foundation
>>shall be laid." ' [1]

The closeness of the relationship between Israel and God, of which all the prophets were convinced, is not lost in Second Isaiah's cosmic theology. It is, indeed, the prophet's combination of intimacy and ultimacy which makes his sense of Israel's vocation so strangely moving:

>For your Maker is your husband,
>>the LORD of hosts is his name;
>and the Holy One of Israel is your Redeemer,
>>the God of the whole earth he is called. [2]

Theoretically, one might suppose, the special relationship of Israel to God ought to have been forgotten when he was seen to be the God of the whole earth. Second Isaiah, however, was not a theorist, but a prophet; he did not think in doctrinal abstractions, but in terms of history. He knew that the whole earth over which God was sovereign was far (as it is still far) from recognizing the fact. Moreover, he was addressing men who believed they had been deserted; his immediate aim was

1. Isa. 44. 24–8; cf. 51. 12–14.   2. Isa. 54. 5.

to convince them that they were still the Chosen People and to show them how their destiny was charged with the greatest possible significance. A choice made by the God of the whole earth was separated by a great gulf from the 'Hobson's Choice' (which was no choice at all) open to the national gods of the surrounding peoples. As a matter of practical and pressing urgency, the danger in which the exiled Jews stood of losing all sense of their vocation had to be matched by an equally great conception of their privilege and responsibility.

Second Isaiah's response to this pastoral problem far exceeded the immediate need and provided the Hebrew-Christian tradition with one of its most profound concepts – that of the 'Servant of the Lord'. It has been customary to start investigations of the meaning of this term by isolating four (or more) oracles of the book – the so-called 'Servant Songs'[1] – and inquiring about the identity of the figure they depict. A bewildering variety of proposals has been made. Since, however, it has never been firmly established that these particular oracles are distinct on grounds of authorship, date of composition or literary style, it is almost certainly a mistake to consider them as isolated 'songs' and thus narrow the evidence to be interpreted. That this approach does narrow the evidence is immediately obvious from the fact that Second Isaiah employs the term 'servant' throughout the whole range of his poems. It is further obvious that, generally speaking, *Israel* is the Servant of the Lord:

> But now hear, O Jacob my servant,
> Israel whom I have chosen!
> Thus says the LORD who made you,
> who formed you from the womb
> and will help you:
> Fear not, O Jacob my servant,
> Jeshurun whom I have chosen.[2]

Here, plainly, Israel is the Servant whom God has chosen to

1. Isa. 42. 1–4; 49. 1–6; 50. 4–9; 52. 13–53. 12. In addition, Isa. 42. 5–9; 49. 8–13 and 51. 9–16 have been thought of as poems belonging to the servant series.

2. Isa. 44. 1–2, where 'Jeshurun' is a poetic term of endearment for Israel; cf. Isa. 41. 8–10; 43. 8–13; 44. 6–8, 21–3; 45. 4.

fulfil his purpose. The main difficulty in the way of maintaining that for Second Isaiah the Servant *always* means Israel is the presentation of the figure as an individual in the so-called 'songs'. Nevertheless, even this strongly individualized presentation does not justify our isolating the 'songs' at the cost of dismembering the series of poems of which they are inextricably a part. If, therefore, we are obliged to affirm that in the thought of Second Isaiah Israel was the Servant, we ought to be aware that we are drawing a conclusion which, whatever it may seem at first glance, is very far from being simple. For into this title has been gathered a wealth of experience and depth of vision, which far transcended the historical community of Israel. It expounded, rather, the mission and destiny *to which Israel was called*:

> The LORD called me from the womb,
>> from the body of my mother he
>>> named my name.
> He made my mouth like a sharp sword,
>> in the shadow of his hand he hid me;
> he made me a polished arrow,
>> in his quiver he hid me away.
> And he said to me, 'You are my servant,
>> Israel, in whom I will be glorified.'
> But I said, 'I have laboured in vain,
>> I have spent my strength for nothing
>>> and vanity;
> yet surely my right is with the LORD,
>> and my recompense with my God.'
>
> And now the LORD says,
>> who formed me from the womb to
>>> be his servant,
> to bring Jacob back to him,
>> and that Israel might be gathered to him,
> for I am honoured in the eyes of the LORD,
>> and my God has become my strength –
> he says:
> 'It is too light a thing that you should
>>> be my servant
>> to raise up the tribes of Jacob
>> and to restore the preserved of Israel;

> I will give you as a light to the nations,
> > that my salvation may reach to the end of
> > > the earth.'[1]

In the personal awareness of her prophetic representative,[2] the magnitude of Israel's responsibility is seen to be commensurate with the magnitude of her privilege. She was called, not for her own salvation only, but for a prophetic mission to the world. She was to be ' a light to the Gentiles'.[3] This glorious charge is the answer to the exiles' despair. The suffering of Israel has been for the nations who despised and rejected her, as soon they will appreciate and confess:

> Surely he has borne *our* griefs
> > and carried *our* sorrows;
> yet we esteemed him stricken,
> > smitten by God, and afflicted.
> But he was wounded for *our* transgressions,
> > he was bruised for *our* iniquities;
> upon him was the chastisement that made *us* whole,
> > and with his stripes *we* are healed.[4]

No Christian can read this poem of victorious suffering and fail to appreciate that it goes beyond the immediate situation of the prophet and his contemporaries and discloses the whole purpose and economy of God. In so far as Israel is the Servant, she is called to become what she is. In so far as the Servant is Israel, it is an Israel the fulness of whose mission and destiny was realized only when the Son of Man ' came not to be served but to serve, and to give his life as a ransom for many'.[5] Second Isaiah's vision of Israel's vocation reaches out to the fulfilment in Christ and his Church.[6]

1. Isa. 49. 1–6.   2. See pp. 51–4.
3. Isa. 42. 6; 44. 5; 45. 6, 14; 51. 4; cf. 45. 20–3.
4. Isa. 53. 4–5.   5. Mark 10. 45.
6. The poems of Second Isaiah are echoed in many passages of the New Testament: Mark 1. 1–3, 11; 14. 24, 65; 15. 15; Matthew 3. 17; 8. 17; 12. 18–21; 26. 67; Luke 22. 37; John 12. 35; 18. 22; 19. 3; Acts 3. 13; 8. 26–39; Romans 15. 21; Philippians 2. 5–11; 1 Peter 2. 24–5.

CHAPTER FOUR

RELIGION AND RIGHTEOUSNESS

In no department of contemporary Christian thinking is the witness of the Hebrew prophets more sorely needed than in that which seeks to understand the relationship between belief and conduct. The recent growth of non-Christian humanism, which pursues morals without religion, has provoked a sharp reaction from many vocal churchmen and led them to ascribe an exaggerated importance to dogmatic orthodoxy.

It is fashionable, but nevertheless foolish, to overlook the obvious fact that non-Christian humanists are capable of upholding high ethical ideals and (to a certain degree) of inspiring men to pursue them in practice. They are quite incapable, however, of providing any release from the heavy burden of guilt which unavoidably follows from human frailty and inevitably inhibits moral effort. Morals without religion are subject, it would appear, to an inexorable law of diminishing returns.

The moral failures of men provide no insoluble problem, on the other hand, to the champions of dogmatic orthodoxy. In theory at least, they are able to relate them to the economy of God and to speak without hesitation of sin and forgiveness. The very precision and confidence with which they present their doctrinal systems are often won, however, at the cost of ignoring the complex issues of ordinary life and it is with these that the humanists (and the bulk of ordinary humanity) are primarily concerned. Although it is true that convictions about fundamental issues, which are ultimately theological, constitute the mainspring of moral action, it is singularly naïve to suppose that intellectual formulations of belief in a cut-and-dried idiom can be (or ever have been) the starting-point of what men actually do.

The humanists are weak just where the dogmatists are strong and vice versa. The good life apart from faith in the living God is an intolerable and impossible burden, and religious dogma abstracted from common human experience is nothing more than a caricature. Both humanist and dogmatist operate in a two-dimensional universe of discourse and conspicuously lack the power which comes from depth. Between them there is so little common ground that discussion is almost impossible and a deadlock has been reached which can only be disastrous for both belief and conduct. It is as futile to attempt to establish the priority of one over the other, as to try to separate and choose between the two sides of a penny. Christian thinkers would do better to recall their neglected prophetic heritage. Israel's great men of God were neither humanists nor dogmatists; and they will convince us that the present impasse really arises from grievous deficiencies in both parties to the conflict.

PERSONAL AND MORAL

In the Hebrew prophets' knowledge of God, religion and morality were perfectly united. The fusion was brought about by their being made aware that the highest element in human experience – moral personality – has its source and fulfilment in the very nature of God himself. It was this awareness which made them alive (as no one else, before Jesus, was alive) to the reality of our human situation. It is worth trying to understand the nature of the prophets' awareness in terms of our own experience – dim and incoherent though it be.

We know from experience that men are 'at their best' in small and intimate communities – like those of the family and groups of personal friends. Here, we are set in a relationship to other people for which the word 'moral' seems too cold a description, although, indeed, we know that it is no less than that. The intimate fusion of reverence and affection of which we are conscious in such fellowships seems at once to safeguard the separateness of each one of us as a person with a life of his own and to ensure that his separateness never declines into lonely isolation. Such reverence-with-affection belongs to the very essence of family life and of friendship. It is also the heart of Christian worship.

Now, if we observe this personal relationship-in-community from the *outside*, we shall be impressed by its standards, its norm of behaviour, its manners, its *mores*. That is what morality means and it is how it came into being. It is a partial (because an external) description of the relationship of persons in community. If, however, we cease to occupy the position of an outside observer and become an integral part of the community, so that we know it from the *inside*, we shall be impressed not so much by its external standards (its morality), as by the quality of its inner life of reverence and affection. For this quality, the highest word is love. Therefore, in using the terms 'morality' and 'love', we are not identifying two different types of relationship, but simply describing the life of persons in community from two different points of view.

If, as we have suggested, morality is born in the mutual relationship of persons in community, we should not be surprised to find that the ethical standards – the *ethos* – of most primitive societies now appear to us to have been much in advance of their religious beliefs. We have great difficulty in acknowledging that men have ever been 'better' than the gods they worshipped, but the evidence allows of no other conclusion. Our reluctance to consider this evidence and to accept its implications shows how much our presuppositions have been shaped by the prophetic tradition of the Bible. Whenever we discover a religion which implies moral standards inferior to those of the society in which it is practised, we may be sure that it is sub-personal. Sometimes, it is sub-personal because it permits an intimacy between the god and his worshippers which eliminates the possibility of reverence. At other times, it is sub-personal because the element of reverence has so far been exaggerated as to erect a barrier between the human and the divine which only magic and ritual can be thought to penetrate. Such a religion ought, in theory, to be irrelevant to the personal conduct of its adherents, but it can hardly ever remain so. Almost inevitably, it influences the morality of those who constantly practise it, and when it does so, it becomes a sanction for sub-human behaviour. The behaviour will be sub-human because it will be determined by a dominant relationship which is sub-personal. Nothing has been (and still can be) so destructive of 'natural' goodness as devotion to a god who is regarded as being less responsible, less trustworthy, and less rational than his worshippers. We recall that the greatest enemy the prophets had to fight was sub-personal religion.

If man is to safeguard and develop his moral awareness in the practice of religion, it is necessary that he should be able to ascribe to God a moral personality akin to his own. But (the question inevitably arises) is it legitimate to conceive of God in terms belonging to our own experience? Would not this be (as Voltaire suggested) to create God in our own image?

The obvious danger of making an idol in our own likeness has sometimes driven religious thinkers to affirm that God is *utterly* different from man. This point of view cannot survive a moment's scrutiny. If it were true, all knowledge of God would be impossible, because, whether we like to admit it or not, it is obvious that God (like everybody and everything) must be understood in terms of our own experience. No religion can dispense with human language; 'anthropomorphism' is a necessity. We must change our question, therefore, and ask: *On what conditions* can human terms be trusted to give a reliable account of the character of God?

The use of categories drawn from human experience for understanding the being and activity of God can be justified ultimately only by the conviction that *God wills to disclose himself to man.* Here, of course, lies the crucial importance of revelation and the prophets' sense of vocation. Their awareness of having been called by God to be his witnesses, their conviction that Israel was deliberately chosen to reveal God's purpose to the world, and, above all, the conviction of the Church of the New Testament that God was in Christ as he lived and lost his human life on earth, give us the assurance that the initiative of revelation was taken by God himself. Only belief in a God who reveals himself to man banishes the suspicion that, in using the language of men, we are merely projecting our own imperfect image on to a god-shaped blank. No such 'projectionist' theory can explain, for instance, why the prophets experienced in their 'calls' a compulsion which ran clean counter to all their natural inclinations, why it was with the words 'Thus says the LORD' that they denounced their contemporaries for inhuman cruelty, and why Christians, who are irrevocably committed to approaching God through an Incarnate Life, are of all men the most conscious of human failure. When, therefore, we draw on our own human experience in order to understand God, we are not simply making a virtue of necessity; *we are using the medium which was chosen by God himself.*

One conclusion from this brief discussion which concerns us immediately is that religious morality ('the will of God') can never outstrip the highest human conception of morality, nor compromise the absolute moral demands of which each man is aware. In maintaining (with all the moralists) that conscience, though fallible, must always be obeyed, we are saying, in effect, that it is through this medium that God makes his will known. The conscience of man is the instrument of the redemptive righteousness of God.

It is, of course, notorious that 'conscientious' people differ among themselves and sometimes to an alarming degree. It is also notorious that the morality sanctified by the Christian tradition has differed very greatly from age to age. If God is absolutely good, how, it may be asked, can such diversity of conduct and conviction in any sense represent *his* will?

It would seem that the 'will of God' cannot be rationalized into any fixed code of behaviour always and everywhere the same, and that the conduct of a single person at any one time has never been (except in the case of Jesus) an adequate index to its nature. Rather, when we use the expression 'the will of God' as an absolute term, we can only mean his will to enter into fellowship with men at *their* best, that is, as moral persons obedient to the voice of conscience. If, however, God demands only the best of which each man is aware at any one time (and no other is possible), what difference can there be between Christian and what thoughtless people call 'secular' morality?

We have already excluded the notion that Christian morality represents the intrusion of some 'wholly other' order into the world of men. The demands of God must obviously be apprehended and worked out in the world by men using their own terms and their own awareness, that is, according to their conscience and their particular circumstances. The difference between this morality and other standards of human conduct arises from the fact that the community of which it is the norm (the *mores*) is not simply a fellowship of human persons, but a fellowship of human persons bound together by their devotion to God in his self-revelation. The conscience of a Christian mediates, that is to say, the personal demands of God-in-Christ, as well as the demands made upon him by men.

The Christian faith, therefore, does not speak of an ideal towards which individuals must strive, nor of a code or a set of principles which they must observe, but of a divine-human society of persons. The personal demands known within this divine-human fellowship penetrate to the inner citadel of our being. Even our 'private' lives cease to be private in communion with him 'unto whom all hearts be open, all desires known, and from whom no secrets are hid'. Moralists have done their best to find a place for motives in their abstract systems; moral theologians have even presumed to weigh men's intentions in the balance; but the heart's sin, which is not carried into act, can assume its full horror only when it is known personally as an offence against God and against the brother for whom Christ died.

EXPERIENCE OF COMMUNITY

Whenever we find morality defined in a code and religion externalized in a cult, we begin to realize that the prophetic faith of the Old and New Testaments has its roots deeper than either. This faith springs from an *inside* knowledge of personal fellowship in the community of God. The meaning of this prophetic communion is no more adequately represented by 'religion-and-doctrine' and 'morality-and-ethics', in isolation the one from the other, than is a poem by two prose paraphrases. No simple addition or conflation of the two can recapture the harmony, the power, and, therefore, the meaning, of their common source. Just as you must be something of a poet to understand poetry, so you must have experience of life in a personal community, before you can begin to understand the personal revelation of God, alike through his servants the prophets, and in Jesus, his Son.

The prophets looked back to the common life of the desert community as their standard of reference, because it was then that Israel was adopted as the family of God. By the time of the prophets, the reverence and affection of those early days had been lost in the impersonal and competitive society of Canaan. That to which the prophets recalled their contemporaries was neither simply a higher morality, nor a purified religion, but the quality of life known in the Exodus community with which God made his covenant.

We shall better understand the prophets' message, if we appreciate, on the one hand, the very close human bonds which were forged in the common life of Israel in the desert, and, on the other hand, the highly concrete and personal conception of God which the prophets inherited from their countrymen. In their different ways, both these factors contributed to the personal and moral core of the prophets' faith. They do not explain it, but without them it could hardly be explained. We shall, therefore, consider each in turn.

The Common Life of the Desert

It is commonly assumed that human dignity depends, principally, on each man's freedom to stand out against his fellows as an independent individual following the imperatives of his 'private' conscience. If, however, there is any truth in our contention that moral personality is the highest value we know and that it is nurtured by life in community, human dignity rests on something different from the flimsy foundation of isolated self-assertion. It rests, rather, on each man's freedom to enjoy the distinctively human privileges of reverence and affection and to fulfil their personal demands.

Romantic notions of the rights of the individual have become so deeply ingrained in our modern presuppositions, that we have almost forgotten that the individual also has his duties. The modern emphasis, in so far as it represents the last vestiges of a worthy conception of men as *persons*, should command our respect, but it is both inadequate in itself and often disastrous in its consequences. When it is isolated and pushed to extremes, the idea that an individual has rights over against his fellows becomes subversive of society and, in consequence, of any kind of moral order.

With this individualistic background, it is not surprising that many students of the Old Testament have been tempted to divide Hebrew religion into two distinct periods. First, it is said, there was a period of tribal collectivism; and, out of that, there emerged the period of prophetic individualism, beginning about the time of Jeremiah. To make this superficial division is to misunderstand both its halves.

The deficiencies of early Hebrew society are great and obvious. When, for example, we read how the innocent family of a guilty person was made to share his punishment, our sense of justice is outraged.[1] In the face of such evidence, it is indeed tempting to pass over the narratives of Israel's early life as supplying data of interest to the anthropologist but irrelevant to any modern concern for religion and righteousness. Other features of early Hebrew tradition suggest, however, that so cavalier a dismissal would be rash in the extreme. For instance, the generous hospitality shown by the desert clan to the isolated wanderer cut off from the protection of his own kindred sheds a very different light on 'primitive' morality.[2] The Israelite tradition carefully preserved this generous attitude to the 'sojourner' (for such was the technical term) and, having characteristically related it to the Exodus deliverance, made it the basis for the duty of treating all weak and defenceless persons with benevolence and respect:

For the LORD your God is God of gods and Lord of lords, the great, the mighty, and the terrible God, who is not partial and takes no bribe. He executes justice for the fatherless and the widow, and loves the sojourner, giving him food and clothing. Love the sojourner therefore; for you were sojourners in the land of Egypt.[3]

The vitality of the desert tradition is similarly demonstrated

1. Josh. 7; Lev. 20. 5; II Kings 9. 26; 21. 10–15; 22. 15–20; II Sam. 21. 1–9; 24; Num. 16. 25–35.
2. Cf. Gen. 18. 1–8; 19. 1–11; Judg. 19. 10–21.
3. Deut. 10. 17–19.

by the constant solicitude for the 'sojourner' which is found in the preaching of the prophets.[1] Historically, we cannot pick and choose between these two features of early Hebrew society – the injustice of group punishment, and the benevolence which accorded rights and privileges to the sojourner. The sojourner gained so much by being received as a 'member of the family', because in ancient Israel 'family feeling' was so tremendously strong. Group punishment and blood revenge, however revolting we find them, spring from precisely this same sense of social solidarity. The early Israelites, like the members of any tribal society, found it easy to believe that they were bound up in a close 'bundle of the living',[2] that a group prospered or suffered misfortune as a whole, because, in fact, this did correspond with the exacting conditions of life in the desert. When, for example, the welfare of a small clan depended upon scanty vegetation and meagre water supplies, its members in the very nature of things developed a strong sense of community. This explains why, in much later times, Old Testament writers still regarded loneliness as the greatest misfortune. It was the curse of Cain.[3] For obvious reasons, therefore, the individual was not sharply differentiated from the group of which he was a member, and, for good or ill, his welfare was identified with that of his fellows.

It would be a mistake, however, to suppose that this emphasis on the life of the community indicated (like godless totalitarianism) an indifference to individual human worth and responsibility. As in the case of the unprotected sojourner, the corporate awareness of the Hebrews was far from excluding the conviction that the individual mattered. The earliest and most characteristic Israelite law addresses each individual member of the community with God's *Thou shalt* and recognizes the humblest man's right to be heard.[4] And even the ancient practice of collective punishment, with all its shortcomings, is not completely devoid of a sense of the individual's

1. Jer. 7. 6; 22. 3; Ezek. 22. 7, 29; Zech. 7. 10; Mal. 3. 5; cf. Deut. 5. 14.
2. 1 Sam. 25. 29; cf. Deut. 21. 1–9.
3. Gen. 4. 11–14; Ps. 102. 7–8; Jer. 15. 17; Hos. 8. 9; Lam. 3. 28.
4. Exod. 20; 22. 21–7; 23. 6; see, further, pp. 105–9.

responsibility. For example, the destruction of Achan's oxen, sheep, and asses, along with his sons and daughters, is explicitly the destruction of 'all that *he* had'.[1] The personal guilt is his. Whatever taint was thought to attach to his family and possessions belonged more to the sphere of ancient psychology than to the sphere of ancient morality. Although, therefore, this strong feeling of solidarity did not necessarily undermine the individual's sense of moral responsibility, the punishment of the innocent with the guilty was eventually seen to be a thing offensive in itself, and voices were raised in protest.[2] The protests became more pronounced about the period of the Exile, because it was then, at one and the same time, that the Jews were deprived of their sense of social solidarity and subjected to collective suffering on a devastating scale. Their resentment found expression in a proverb: 'The fathers have eaten sour grapes, and the children's teeth are set on edge.'[3] No doubt this popular and pithy summary of orthodox teaching was used as much as an excuse as a protest; it proclaimed the exiles' innocence. In order to remove their resentment and provoke them to penitence, it would appear that the exiles were taught an extreme form of individualism, such as we find in the book of Ezekiel.[4] It is important to appreciate that the legalistic and atomistic theory advanced in Ezekiel, so far from representing the triumphant emergence of the individual from a 'mass' society, is an aberration which is confirmed neither by human experience nor the rest of the Old Testament. As the book of Job was to show, the problem of innocent suffering is not solved by denying its possibility. It is easy, therefore, to attach too much importance to this evidence for 'individualism'; generally speaking, what was good in it was already old and what was new in it was wrong.

When the prophets addressed society as a whole,[5] they were

1. Josh. 7. 24.
2. Deut. 24. 16; II Sam. 24. 17; II Kings 14. 6; Num. 16. 22. The alternative to collective punishment in Gen. 18. 23–33 is not individual retribution, but *collective salvation*.
3. Jer. 31. 29; Ezek. 18. 2; cf. Lam. 5. 7.
4. Ezek. 3. 17–21; 14. 12–23; 18. 1–32; 33. 1–20; cf. Jer. 31. 29–30.
5. E.g. Amos 3. 1; Jer. 7. 23; see, further, p. 55.

upholding the conviction that God had called Israel to be a *people*, a community in which he had set individuals in a new relationship to each other by their new relationship to himself. The ancient sense of social solidarity was, therefore, not abandoned in Israel, but established on firmer foundations, whose builder and maker was God.

The Common Life of God and Man

It is dangerous to talk of a kinship between God and man, unless we realize at the outset that we can do so only because God wills that men should understand his nature and purpose. If God had willed simply and solely to be God and not God-*to-us*, he would merely be the object of philosophical speculation or superstitious awe. The belief that God is personal and has disclosed himself to man is the basic conviction of the whole Bible. We are justified, therefore, in speaking of the *revealed* kinship between God and man.

This kinship is fully and completely manifested in the life of Jesus, but it is partially revealed in the faith of the Old Testament. Nowhere is the common life of God and man so joyously affirmed as in the imaginative world of Hebrew metaphor, where quite unconsciously the men of Israel were preparing mankind for the Incarnation – the Word made flesh. We are able to apprehend God as active and personal, largely because the Old Testament writers never for a moment allowed any other thought to cross their minds. This alone would be sufficient reason for asserting that the Hebrew scriptures are indispensable for the nurture of Christian faith. What, then, is their secret?

The Hebrews, like all other primitive peoples, were quite incapable of appreciating abstract ideas. Beneath most of the nouns of the Old Testament, there throbs a living verb. More often than not, it invites you to wander in an Israelite community and observe its everyday life. One might almost say that Hebrew religion is a religion of the verb rather than the noun, because it finds its characteristic expression in *action*. This constitutes its moral strength and it helps to illuminate the fact that the self-revelation of God in the Old Testament is given in the history of the life of a people and not in doctrinal propositions.

From the very beginning, the Israelites conceived of God as a personal being, whom they described in a riot of metaphor – and on such a scale that is possible to build up an almost complete picture of Hebrew society from the images they put to theological use. Christians have become so accustomed to a small selection of these metaphors (like King and Judge), that they have tended to interpret them too literally and use them as something like 'verbal photographs'. It is easy to forget that they belong, not to the world of exact representation or precise definition, but to the world of poetic imagination – a world in which language is treated with such impropriety that the little hills rejoice and the valleys laugh and sing.[1]

Many of our best popular hymns have their roots in this rich soil of poetic awareness. They can, therefore, prepare us to recapture something of the world from which the prophets speak. For example, the familiar hymn of Newton, which begins 'How sweet the name of Jesus sounds', conveys a clear meaning, while at the same time absolutely forbidding a prosaic and pedestrian interpretation:

> Jesus! my Shepherd, Husband, Friend,
> My Prophet, Priest, and King,
> My Lord, my Life, my Way, my End,
> Accept the praise I bring.

It is when, as in this verse, metaphors are mixed with so careless a rapture, that we learn to understand the (limited) contribution of each one of them in its proper poetic context. We must approach most of the poetic oracles of the prophets in exactly the same way.

No Old Testament writer took thought before speaking of God. That is why every page of the Hebrew scriptures abounds in imagery, which (to our literalistic Western minds) is quite bewildering. For example, God's relationship to his people is represented under the figures of a father,[2] mother,[3] brother,[4]

1. Ps. 65. 12–13.   2. Jer. 3. 19.   3. Deut. 32. 18.
4. Isa. 36. 3 (Joah = Yah(weh) is brother).

husband,[1] friend,[2] warrior,[3] shepherd,[4] farmer,[5] metal-worker,[6] builder,[7] potter,[8] fuller,[9] physician,[10] judge,[11] water-seller,[12] king,[13] and scribe[14] – to mention, almost at random, a few of the relationships and activities of the people's common life. The relative rarity of impersonal metaphors distinguishes the God of Israel from the gods of the nations, who are regularly likened to birds and animals. The kinship of the God of Israel is with human persons.

When the Hebrews claimed that their God was the *living God*,[15] they meant what they said and demonstrated in their theological method the courage of their convictions. They displayed no reticence, for example, in ascribing to him the most human of emotions, like repentance, indignation, impatience, pain, exultation, sorrow, compassion, joy, anger, vengeance, scorn, hatred, and love. Such a list could be extended almost indefinitely, but it will serve its purpose if it suggests that we fall into ludicrous errors, when we select one or two of these metaphors and then proceed to interpret them as precise and formal theological terms.

It is obvious enough that some of this language suggests a conception of God which falls short of the best we know in ordinary human experience, but we must be very clear about what features of it we ought to reject. Too often, theologians have relegated nearly the whole of it to the nursery and Sunday School as 'childish anthropomorphism' or 'mere metaphor', as if to suggest that the adult mind can dispense with the use of analogy. Such sophistication is pitiful self-deception. Metaphor – *mere* metaphor – is all we have to help us communicate (both to ourselves and others) our understanding of God, no matter how discreetly we try to disguise the fact by organizing a selection of images into a system of doctrinal propositions. Such figures as the 'fatherhood' of God, the 'kingship' of God, the 'wrath' of God, the 'love' of God,

---

1. Hos. 2. 16.
2. Jer. 3. 4.
3. Isa. 63. 1–2.
4. Ezek. 34. 31.
5. Amos 9. 9.
6. Ezek. 22. 20.
7. Amos 7. 7.
8. Isa. 45. 9.
9. Isa. 4. 4; cf. Jer. 2. 22.
10. Deut. 32. 39.
11. Isa. 33. 22.
12. Isa. 55. 1–2.
13. Jer. 10. 10.
14. Jer. 31. 33.
15. Jer. 10. 10; 23. 36; Pss. 18. 46; 42. 2; II Sam. 12. 5; 14. 11; 15. 21.

and all the rest remain metaphorical, because they were and still are at some point anchored to human experience. They would be incomprehensible (and, therefore, useless) if they were not. If only we could stop dehydrating the poetry of the Bible and discover once again that it provides a 'sacramental' approach to the common ways of God and man, our account of Biblical revelation would be purged of some of the shrivelled and lifeless language with which it is at present encumbered. Our preaching might then become at once more personal, more imaginative, and more intelligible. At the present time, it really does seem that Christians are desperately afraid of straying from the well-trodden path of sanctified jargon and of claiming that measure of freedom to venture theologically which all the great preachers – from Amos to St Paul – assumed, not as a novel stunt, but as a pastoral and spiritual necessity.

In the world of Hebrew poetry, God and man lived a common life. It was in this community of experience, which the Old Testament writers always took for granted, that God was known as personal and, therefore, as akin to man. The prophets, however, expressed their conviction with even greater concreteness. They affirmed that God had called Israel into a relationship of personal intimacy in order that man might be restored to his place in the life of God's family.

The notion of family kinship is never far from the surface of the prophets' great metaphor of redemption. When, for example, Second Isaiah described God as Israel's Redeemer,[1] he was using a term which bore witness to the solidarity of family life. In Israel, a redeemer was the next-of-kin, who restored the wholeness of his family by the 'redemption' of what properly belonged to it, such, for example, as one of its members from slavery. Therefore, to redeem a person was to act as his kinsman and claim him as your own.[2] The prophets – of all people – cannot be accused of underestimating the extent to which man had obscured this basic kinship by sin, but they could hardly have made their passionate appeals for

1. See p. 84 and compare Job 19. 25.
2. Isa. 43. 1; 44. 23; 48. 20; 52. 9; 59. 20; 60. 16; cf. Lev. 25. 47–9; Ruth 3. 12–13; 4. 1–6.

moral and spiritual reformation, had they not believed that God had made man in his own image for fellowship with himself.[1]

Israel's highly concrete and personal conception of God was, perhaps, occasionally coloured by oriental exaggeration, but it had the inestimable advantage of being directly related to the real world of common experience. The prophets knew that discrimination was necessary and were acutely aware of the severe limitations of all human language for conveying the truth about one who was 'God and not man.'[2] The criterion of their discrimination, however, was not (as too often with us) a fearful and deadening sophistication, of the kind which urges that God may be described only in negatives. It was, rather, an insight into the nature of God as personal and moral. What they rejected was not (if the loose phrase may be allowed) the 'humanity' of God, but everything which suggested that he was capricious and unworthy of human insight at its best.

RIGHTEOUSNESS

The prophets were convinced that they had been called by God to stand in his intimate council.[3] There they learnt that he deals with men as a man deals with his friends – in a word, that he is personal and moral. It followed that nothing which offended the enlightened human conscience could any longer be thought 'religious', and that the primary way in which God could be 'known' was the way in which men know each other – by personal and moral sensitiveness in the ordinary ways of life. The faith of the prophets was nothing if not practical, and the practice they demanded of their countrymen over two thousand five hundred years ago is still found to be binding on the Christian conscience. Our moral awareness

1. Gen. 1. 26; Ps. 8.
2. Hos. 11. 9; Isa. 31. 3; 45. 9–12; 55. 8–9; Jer. 17. 5; cf. Job 10. 4–6; 34. 10–15; Gen. 6. 3; 11 Chron. 32. 8; Pss. 103. 14–18; 139.6; Num. 23. 19; 1 Kings 8. 27.
3. See pp. 45f.

in the twentieth century has been considerably dimmed by the impersonal life of a suburbanized society and weakened by a type of religious teaching which has lost its impact in becoming dogmatic. The Christian conscience needs a new freedom and a new power. It may rediscover both alongside these servants of God, as they speak out to their own day without fear or favour.

The Righteousness of the Prophets

'The LORD sent Nathan to David.' With these words, the curtain rises on one of the most exquisite and effective narratives in the Old Testament.[1] David, you may remember, is told by the prophet how a poor man had been callously deprived of his solitary ewe lamb:

> There were two men in a certain city, the one rich and the other poor. The rich man had very many flocks and herds; but the poor man had nothing but one little ewe lamb, which he had bought. And he brought it up, and it grew up with him and with his children; it used to eat of his morsel, and drink from his cup, and lie in his bosom, and it was like a daughter to him. Now there came a traveller to the rich man, and he was unwilling to take one of his own flock or herd to prepare for the wayfarer who had come to him, but he took the poor man's lamb, and prepared it for the man who had come to him.[2]

David fell into Nathan's trap and, in roundly condemning the rich man 'because he had no pity,' passed judgement on his own theft of Bathsheba from Uriah, her lawful husband. Little did the king expect the devastating climax: 'Nathan said to David, "You are the man."'

This story gives us the flavour of the prophets' moral sensitiveness and a hint of their extraordinary courage. Also from the early prophetic tradition comes the comparable story of how Elijah championed the cause of one of Ahab's subjects, when the king's notorious wife, Jezebel, murdered him to get possession of his vineyard. The narrative makes it clear that much more than a theory of private property or a dispute about compensation was involved:

1. II Sam. 12. 1–15.   2. II Sam. 12. 1–4.

Now Naboth the Jezreelite had a vineyard in Jezreel, beside the palace of Ahab king of Samaria. And after this Ahab said to Naboth, 'Give me your vineyard, that I may have it for a vegetable garden, because it is near my house; and I will give you a better vineyard for it; or, if it seems good to you, I will give you its value in money.' But Naboth said to Ahab, 'The LORD forbid that I should give you the inheritance of my fathers.' And Ahab went into his house vexed and sullen because of what Naboth the Jezreelite had said to him; for he had said, 'I will not give you the inheritance of my fathers.' And he lay down on his bed, and turned away his face, and would eat no food.[1]

The man who wrote this account clearly had a deep loathing for the type of prosperous vulgarian who thinks that he can buy out a man's self-respect. In Israel, a man's family property was reckoned an integral part of himself,[2] and the narrator was concerned to show how the prophet upheld what we should call 'the sanctity of personality' against interference even from the head of the state. The large-scale confiscation of property in the eighth and seventh centuries B.C. shows how the covenant tradition of equality and brotherhood learned in the desert had been smashed by the new 'civilized' standards of the kingdom.[3] The prophets strenuously denounced all such grabbing, because it manifested a fundamental indifference to the dignity of human persons. Hear Micah on the subject:

> Woe to those who devise wickedness
> and work evil upon their beds!
> When the morning dawns, they perform it,
> because it is in the power of their hand.
> They covet fields, and seize them;
> and houses, and take them away;
> they oppress a man and his house,
> a man and his inheritance.[4]

Because it is in the power of their hand. Micah's condemnation of this free enterprise society is more than an economic judge-

1. 1 Kings 21. 1–4.
2. Jer. 32. 6–12; Lev. 25. 25–34; Ezek. 46. 16–18.
3. 1 Sam. 8. 14–15; Jer. 22. 13–19; Deut. 17. 14–17.
4. Mic. 2. 1–2; cf. 2. 8–9; Isa. 2. 7; 3. 14; 5. 8; Amos 4. 1; Exod. 20. 17.

ment. His sense of outrage springs from an appreciation of the human situation in its fundamental divine and personal dimensions. The righteousness of the prophet is the righteousness of God himself.

It is abundantly clear that the people of God had accepted the debased standards of a competitive society and had lost the personal integrity which their forefathers had learnt in the days of Moses. Small and eccentric groups – like the Rechabites and Nazirites – still clung conservatively to parts of the nomadic tradition, but they were too withdrawn from ordinary society to exercise any general influence.[1] Their escapist 'return-to-the-desert' ideal resembles the arty-craftiness of some modern attempts to return to the homespun life of the Middle Ages. Much as the prophets upheld the standards of nomad Israel,[2] their cry was not simply 'Return to the desert', but 'Return to the God of the Exodus.' They alone effectively revolted against the corruption and cruelty which cried to high heaven on every side.

The eighth century B.C. in its earlier phase had been enjoying a post-war boom almost without precedent. Damascus in the north and Assyria to the far north-east were too busily preoccupied with their own concerns to interfere in Israel's national life. The period from about 785 to 745 B.C. was therefore a veritable gala-time for the ambitious and the unprincipled *nouveaux riches*. The reaction of Amos is characteristic:

> Woe to those who are at ease in Zion,
>   and to those who feel secure on the
>   mountain of Samaria,
> the notable men of the first of the nations,
>   to whom the house of Israel come!
> O you who put far away the evil day,
>   and bring near the seat of violence [!]
> Woe to those who lie upon beds of ivory,
>   and stretch themselves upon their couches,
> and eat lambs from the flock,
>   and calves from the midst of the stall;

1. Jer. 35. 1–19; II Kings 10. 15–28; Num. 6. 1–21; Amos 2. 11–12.
2. Jer. 2. 2–3; Hos. 2. 15; 9. 10; 11. 1–2.

who sing idle songs to the sound of the harp,
    and like David invent for themselves
        instruments of music;
who drink wine in bowls,
    and anoint themselves with the finest oils,
    but are not grieved over the ruin of Joseph!
Therefore they shall now be the first of those
        to go into exile,
    and the revelry of those who stretch themselves shall
        pass away.[1]

These idle sprawlers, luxuriating in their choice lamb and veal – especially fattened ('from the midst of the stall'), improvising their decadent music, pickling themselves in alcohol (taking it not by the cup but by the bowl), and regaling themselves with the finest cosmetics, as though they had something to celebrate, are pilloried here with unsurpassed invective. They will be the first, says Amos, to suffer in the coming judgement of the nation, which their feckless indifference has hastened.

The prophets were violent, because they lived in a world where honesty and decency were being violated every day. They could not profess a vocation from the Lord, the God of righteousness, and stand aloof when disgusting luxury was being purchased at the price of the blood of the defenceless poor:

For wicked men are found among my people;
    they lurk like fowlers lying in wait.
They set a trap;
    they catch men.
Like a basket full of birds,
    their houses are full of treachery;
therefore they have become great and rich,
    they have grown fat and sleek.
They know no bounds in deeds of wickedness;
    they judge not with justice
the cause of the fatherless, to make it prosper,
    and they do not defend the rights
        of the needy.

1. Amos 6. 1, 3–7; cf. 2. 6–7; 4. 1–3; 5. 10–13; Isa. 1. 23; 3. 16–4. 1; 5. 8–13.

> Shall I not punish them for these things?
>> says the LORD,
> and shall I not avenge myself
> on a nation such as this?[1]

It was only too easy in the times of the prophets to swindle the helpless,[2] to exploit human want by usury,[3] to get away with sharp-practice in business dealings (underweighing and over-charging),[4] to murder and rob,[5] and then to evade punishment by bribing the judges.[6] A man's word was too light a thing to be allowed to stand in the way of ambition and greed.[7]

The fearlessness with which the prophets let their conscience speak against this travesty of human conduct reveals the quality of their moral awareness. It had been informed and empowered by their personal knowledge of God in a manner which was quite without precedent:

> The LORD enters into judgement
>> with the elders and princes of his people:
> 'It is you who have devoured the vineyard,
>> the spoil of the poor is in your houses.
> What do you mean by crushing my people,
>> by grinding the face of the poor?'
>> says the Lord GOD of hosts.[8]

Isaiah's 'social conscience' sprang from his faith. That is why he used the expression '*my* people', as if to say, 'as you did it to one of the least of these my brethren, you did it to me.'[9] For the prophets, inhuman cruelty was nothing less than religious apostasy, because it disrupted the family life of God's people and denied the sovereignty of the Righteous One. What they found in society was not only cruelty, but cruelty

1. Jer. 5. 26–9.
2. Amos 5. 11; Mic. 3. 1–3; Ezek. 22. 29; Mal. 3. 5; Isa. 10. 1–2.
3. Ezek. 18. 10–13; 22. 12; Hab. 2. 6–7; Exod. 22. 25–7; Deut. 23. 19–20.
4. Amos 8. 4–6; Deut. 25. 13–16.
5. Hos. 4. 1–3; 6. 8–9; 7. 1; Isa. 1. 21; Jer. 7. 9–10; Ezek. 7. 23; 9. 9; 11. 6.
6. Amos 5. 12; 6. 12; Mic. 3. 9–11; Isa. 5. 22–3; 10. 1–2; Zeph. 3. 3.
7. Hos. 4. 1–2; Jer. 34. 8–17.   8. Isa. 3. 14–15.
9. Matthew 25. 40.

masquerading under the cloak of piety. Jeremiah, perhaps more than any other member of the goodly fellowship, was literally appalled by such hypocrisy:

> Will you steal, murder, commit adultery, swear falsely, burn incense to Baal, and go after other gods that you have not known, and then come and stand before me in this house, which is called by my name, and say, 'We are delivered!' – only to go on doing all these abominations? Has this house, which is called by my name, become a den of robbers in your eyes? Behold, I myself have seen it, says the LORD.[1]

With comparable horror, Amos exposed the licentious indulgence which passed for religious observance at Israel's local sanctuaries:

> a man and his father go in to the
> same maiden,
> so that my holy name is profaned;
> they lay themselves down beside every altar
> upon garments taken in pledge;
> and in the house of their God they drink
> the wine of those who have been fined.[2]

Such piety was damnable and the prophets' exposure of it was never forgotten. More than five hundred years later, the author of the book Ecclesiasticus wrote in very much the same vein:

> He that sacrificeth of a thing wrongfully gotten,
> his offering is made in mockery;
> And the mockeries of wicked men are not well-pleasing.
> The Most High hath no pleasure in the offerings of
> the ungodly;
> Neither is he pacified for sins by the multitude
> of sacrifices.
> As one that killeth the son before his father's eyes
> Is he that bringeth a sacrifice from the goods of the poor.[3]

The stark contrast between men's rebellion against God by inhumanity to their fellows and their enthusiastic performance of the rites of sacrificial worship completely revolted the

1. Jer. 7. 9–11.
2. Amos 2. 7–8; cf. Hos. 4. 14; Deut. 23. 17; Exod. 22. 26–7.
3. Ecclesiasticus 34. 18–20; cf. Prov. 21. 3, 27.

prophets. It clearly showed that such worship was in no sense whatsoever an outward and visible sign of an inward and spiritual communion: 'thou art near in their mouth and far from their heart.'[1] Although it must in fairness be said that we have no reason to suppose that everybody who practised sacrifice was a contemptible formalist, or that the life of all Israelite sanctuaries was devoid of spiritual significance, the evidence suggests that in the eighth and seventh centuries B.C. the cult was very deeply paganized. Israel's trouble was not a lack of religion, but an excess of it. As aspirins comfort the man with toothache, sacrificial worship was a palliative, not removing the evil, but numbing the awareness, a magic drug of which the efficacy was automatic, *ex opere operato*. It is not surprising, therefore, that whenever the great prophets speak of sacrifice, their words burn with indignation and loathing: 'For God's sake, stop it!' That was their message.[2]

Curious students of the prophetic writings have not been content to leave the matter there. Granted, they say, that the prophets condemned the abuse of sacrifice, did they also condemn sacrifice in itself and wish to abolish it entirely? The ensuing debate has generated more heat than light. It seems that the argument will never be concluded, for the simple reason that the distinction between sacrifice as practised and sacrifice in itself is not a distinction which would have occurred to the prophets. When we press the theoretical question, all our evidence is indirect and, therefore, ambiguous. What is quite unambiguous is the fact that the cult they saw before their very eyes they whole-heartedly detested. Our efforts to reduce their denunciations to a neat formula – either 'The sacrificial system must be reformed' or 'The sacrificial system must be abolished' – appear to be misguided. Those who maintain that the prophets could not have intended any more than the reform of the debased worship of the sanctuaries, because it is impossible to conceive how Israel's worship could have continued without sacrifice in one form or another, must find more compelling reasons for their confidence.

1. Jer. 12. 2; cf. Isa. 29. 13; Mark 7. 6–7.
2. Amos 4. 4–5; 5. 21–4; Hos. 6. 6; 8. 11–13; Isa. 1. 10–17; Mic. 6. 6–8; Jer. 6. 20; 7. 21–8; Isa. 66. 1–4; 1 Sam. 15. 22.

Both Amos and Jeremiah flatly claimed (whether rightly or wrongly is wholly irrelevant) that sacrifice was no part of Israel's worship in the days of Moses;[1] after the fall of Jerusalem, the Jews of the dispersion worshipped without sacrifice; and the Christian Church repudiated it.[2] It is hardly possible to maintain, therefore, that animal sacrifice is an essential part even of Jewish religion. Nor is it possible to attach much importance to the prophets' failure to propose an alternative to the normal cultus, since none of them was an ecclesiastical planner and many of them, in any case, believed that the people had little future to plan for. The abolition of sacrifice (if that had been their aim) would have been a comparatively insignificant breach with the national tradition alongside the destruction of the nation itself.

The confident anti-abolitionists sometimes lean on the fact that the prophetic oracles were preserved by a post-exilic tradition which not only accepted sacrifice, but found in it genuine joy and delight. This line of argument assumes that the editors of the Hebrew scriptures never allowed anything of which they themselves did not thoroughly approve to slip through their fingers. This assumption cannot survive a moment's scrutiny of the evidence. Nobody who pauses to consider the conflicting regulations of the law books, the astonishing combinations in the Psalter, the contradictory narratives which have been allowed to stand in the historical books, and the retention of incidents discreditable to Israel's heroes, will find himself able to subscribe to any theory of editorial censorship or editorial tidiness in the making of the Old Testament. It is therefore by no means certain that the prophets must have shared the views of the men who collected and preserved their oracles.

Indeed, in the whole of this highly theoretical controversy, nothing is certain. What is sure and very revealing is the prophets' spontaneous and vigorous repudiation of the practice current in their day. It is not only what they said which carries weight, but the utterly scornful indignation with which they said it; as, for example, when Jeremiah lumps together

1. Amos 5. 25; Jer. 7. 22.
2. Hebrews 10. 4–9; Mark 12. 28–34; Matthew 9. 10–13; 12. 1–8.

the burnt offerings, which were not eaten by the worshippers, with those that were and tells the people (since God is not interested) to eat the whole lot themselves: 'Add your burnt offerings to your sacrifices, and eat the flesh.'[1] Even more significant, however, is the fact that when the prophets attack the cult, they explicitly contrast it with their own unambiguous understanding of what is really meant by devotion and obedience to God:

> What to me is the multitude of
> > your sacrifices?
> > says the LORD;
> I have had enough of burnt offerings
> > of rams
> > and the fat of fed beasts;
> I do not delight in the blood of bulls,
> > or of lambs, or of he-goats.
>
> When you come to appear before me,
> > who requires of you
> > this trampling of my courts?
> Bring no more vain offerings;
> > incense is an abomination to me.
> New moon and sabbath and the calling
> > of assemblies –
> > I cannot endure iniquity and
> > solemn assembly.
> Your new moons and your appointed feasts
> > my soul hates;
> they have become a burden to me,
> > I am weary of bearing them.
> When you spread forth your hands,
> > I will hide my eyes from you;
> even though you make many prayers,
> > I will not listen;
> > your hands are full of blood.
> Wash yourselves; make yourselves clean;
> > remove the evil of your doings
> > from before my eyes;
> cease to do evil,
> > learn to do good;

1. Jer. 7. 21; compare the irony of Amos 4. 4–5.

> seek justice,
>> correct oppression;
> defend the fatherless,
>> plead for the widow.[1]

The service which God demands is *righteousness of life*. If we
believe that the prophets' emphasis was mistaken, it is better
to admit it without prevarication than to smudge their convictions in order that we may continue to walk in their company. It is evident, however, that at least some Israelite
circles accepted and developed an interpretation of the prophets' teaching which caused uneasiness about the cultus. It
is reflected in more than one passage of the Psalter:

> Hear, O my people, and I will speak,
>> O Israel, I will testify against you.
>> I am God, your God.
> I do not reprove you for your sacrifices;
>> your burnt offerings are continually before me.
> I will accept no bull from your house,
>> nor he-goat from your folds.
> For every beast of the forest is mine,
>> the cattle on a thousand hills.
> I know all the birds of the air,
>> and all that moves in the field is mine.
>
> If I were hungry, I would not tell you;
>> for the world and all that is in it is mine.
> Do I eat the flesh of bulls,
>> or drink the blood of goats?
> Offer to God a sacrifice of thanksgiving,
>> and pay your vows to the Most High;
> and call upon me in the day of trouble;
>> I will deliver you, and you shall glorify me.[2]

This calm exposition of the futility of animal holocausts is
perhaps more conclusive than the prophets' unrestrained invective. If they themselves did not explore the implications of
the message they were given to proclaim, it has yet to be established that the psalmist did not correctly interpret its ultimate
meaning.

1. Isa. 1. 11–17; compare the same contrast in most of the passages
listed on p. 111, n. 2, and see Exod. 19. 5.
2. Ps. 50. 7–15; cf. Pss. 40. 6–8; 51. 15–17; Isa. 40. 16; 58. 3–9.

The Righteousness of the Lord

When the message of the Hebrew prophets began to stimulate new interest in the last century, it was almost inevitable that it should have been interpreted primarily as a call for social righteousness. Such was the temper of the times. As we have seen, the prophets strongly emphasized this demand of true religion in their outspoken preaching and what they said in the eighth and seventh centuries B.C. is still very much to the point. It is necessary to insist, however, that the prophets' 'social gospel' was rooted and grounded in God. Their moral insight and power are inexplicable apart from their religion.

As soon as we begin to use the word 'religion' in speaking of the prophets, the suspicion arises that it is not a very happy way of describing their characteristic faith. We need a term which makes it clear that 'religion', as they conceived it, was not a special department of life, for which some few people are equipped by their having been endowed with a particular kind of temperament. The prophets did not try to lead a 'religious revival' and their reasons for not doing so are worth consideration in the middle of the twentieth century. What they were concerned to do was to uphold the moral and spiritual life of the whole community – the community which God himself had called into being, and in which he could be *known* by the reverence and affection of its members for each other. Thus, for example, Jeremiah could say of Josiah:

> He judged the cause of the poor and needy;
>> then it was well.
> Is not this to *know* me?
>> says the LORD.[1]

Righteousness was not a duty imposed by religion; it *was* religion, the way, that is to say, of knowing and serving God. The best method of exploring this prophetic understanding of religion is to investigate what they meant by the righteousness of the Lord.

Basically, the term 'righteous' (*çédheq*) means that which is regarded as being standard and normal. Thus, for example,

---

1. Jer. 22. 16.

it was used to describe 'just' or standard weights and measures.¹ To be 'righteous' means, therefore, to conform with the accepted standard, to be 'in the right'. Fundamentally, the term is a legal and not a moral one, as is obvious from the fact that you are 'put in the right' (but not, of course, made *morally* righteous) when a wrong is committed against you.² Now, it is the business of a judge to decide in disputed cases who is 'in the right'. By dispensing justice, he maintains the *norm* of society; in giving judgement, he declares one party 'guilty' and the other party 'innocent' – by reference, always, to the *normal* standard (the law). It is clear that justice ('rightness') and the judgements by which it is expressed and maintained are closely related, and more obviously so in a society where law is little more than uncodified custom. It is not surprising, therefore, that the Hebrew term for the judgement or legal decision (*mishpāṭ*) pronounced by a judge (*shôphēṭ*) is also used in the Old Testament to mean the 'done thing', the customary manner of life in a community, or (more generally) what has been accepted as right and fitting.³

A particular manner of life was right and fitting for Israel with whom God had entered into an intimate covenant relationship. The norm of this new community was not merely traditional social custom, but the character and will of God who brought it into being. The righteousness which the prophets demand is invariably the righteousness of the Lord.⁴ The contrast between the righteousness which God expected of his people and the rebellion he suffered from them is forcefully stated in the climax of Isaiah's 'Song of the Vineyard':

> For the vineyard of the LORD of hosts
> is the house of Israel,
> and the men of Judah
> are his pleasant planting;
> and he looked for justice (*mishpāṭ*),
> but behold, bloodshed (*mispāḥ*);

1. Ezek. 45. 10; Deut. 25. 15; Lev. 19. 36.
2. Ezek. 16. 51–2; Gen. 38. 26; 1 Sam. 24. 17.
3. 1 Kings 18. 28; II Kings 17. 33; Judg. 13. 12; 18. 7; 1 Sam. 27. 11; Exod. 26. 30; 1 Kings 6. 38.
4. Jer. 9. 23–4; Hos. 2. 19; 10. 12; Isa. 28. 17; Zeph. 3. 5.

for righteousness (*çedhāqāh*)
    but behold, a cry (*çeʿāqāh*).[1]

This powerful play on words can hardly be represented in English. God expected morality and found murder, riotousness instead of righteousness.

When, in the prophetic books, we read that 'the LORD has a controversy with his people,'[2] legal language is again being used. The image is that of a court of law before which Israel stands accused; sometimes God is the plaintiff, more often he is the Judge. The judgements he delivers not only condemn evil-doers[3] but also (and at the same time) vindicate the oppressed, which is in line with the fact that to 'judge' the oppressed in the Old Testament always means to deliver them.[4]

God, however, was more than the Judge of Israel; he was Judge of the whole world.[5] This prophetic conviction is clear in the first two chapters of Amos, which make a tremendous sweep through the nations on Israel's borders – Damascus, the Philistines, Tyre, Edom, Ammon, Moab – pronouncing doom on each for its notorious conduct and finally coming home with accumulated momentum to condemn Israel herself.[6] Similarly, Isaiah, who shared Amos' conviction that his own people was on trial in the divine court, also affirms that God's judgement will be pronounced on the arrogant boasting of the king of Assyria.[7] Second Isaiah, therefore, had good precedent in the prophetic tradition for representing Israel's God as Judge of all the earth. In his time, the case to be decided was no longer one between the innocent and guilty within Israel, but one between Israel and her external oppressors. In a series of trial scenes,[8] the nations are summoned to appear before the divine Judge:

> Listen to me in silence, O coastlands;
>   let the peoples renew their strength;
> let them approach, then let them speak;
>   let us together draw near for judgement.

1. Isa. 5. 7.
2. Mic. 6. 2; cf. Hos. 4. 1; Isa. 1. 2–4; 3. 13; Jer. 2. 9.
3. Ezek. 7. 3; 11. 10.   4. Isa. 1. 17, 23; Jer. 22. 16; Ps. 72. 4.
5. Gen. 18. 25.   6. Amos 1. 3–2. 16.
7. Isa. 10. 12–16; 14. 24–7; 37. 22–9.
8. Isa. 41. 1–42. 4; 43. 8–13; 45. 20–5; 50. 8–9.

> Behold, all who are incensed against you
>   shall be put to shame and confounded;
> those who strive against you
>   shall be as nothing and shall perish.
> You shall seek those who contend with you,
>   but you shall not find them;
> those who war against you
>   shall be as nothing at all.
> For I, the LORD your God,
>   hold your right hand;
> it is I who say to you, 'Fear not,
>   I will help you.'[1]

The essential point to grasp is that, for the prophets, the righteousness of the Lord found expression both in judgement on wickedness and in salvation from wickedness. Just as the early leaders of Israel are called judges and saviours, so God is declared to be a 'righteous God and a Saviour'.[2] He is both at the same time and for the same reason. His righteousness is manifested in the acts by which he brought Israel into being, when he called her out of Egypt,[3] the acts by which he condemns wicked offenders against his moral order as embodied in the life of the faithful among his people, and the acts by which he delivers his people from the nations who seek to destroy her.[4] No other term so fully expresses the character and purpose of God and the ultimate significance for the world of Israel's life and history.

The word 'righteousness', of course, only provides a framework of reference and in itself tells us nothing about the content of God's revealed character and purpose. That we must discover by observing its specific manifestations in the story of Israel. It is, however, most illuminating to find that the prophets are able to use this one term to describe (a) the purposeful activity of God in history; (b) the moral 'law' of the universe; and (c) the source and goal of Israel's unique vocation. It means, in other words, that they were quite unaware of our

1. Isa. 41. 1, 11–13.   2. Judg. 2. 16; 3. 9–10; Isa. 45. 21.
3. Exod. 6. 6; 7. 4; cf. Mic. 6. 5; Ps. 103. 6–7; Judg. 5. 11; 1 Sam. 12. 7; Isa. 45. 24.
4. Isa. 41. 10; 45. 8; 46. 13; 51. 5; 62. 11; cf. Isa. 11. 4–5; Jer. 23. 6; Hos. 2. 19; Mic. 7. 9.

distinction between religion and ethics, the service of God and the service of our fellow men. When the prophet devoted himself to righteousness, he devoted himself to God, the good of his neighbour, and the good of the community as the family of God. In the terms of prophetic faith, you simply cannot be moral without serving and revealing God; you cannot be 'godly' without serving your neighbour; and you cannot serve the community without being both moral *and* 'godly'.

We can trace the same fundamental inter-relationship in the prophets' conception of the opposite of righteousness – sin. Outside the prophetic tradition, sin was primarily an offence against God's holiness and many so-called sins were little more than breaches of a taboo. Like the 'unwitting' sins described in the post-exilic law books (but, perhaps, derived from ancient tradition), they are devoid of anything we easily recognize as morally significant.[1] The prophets, however, radically departed from this whole outlook. They declared that what principally constituted sin against God was man's cruelty to man. When a man treated his neighbour callously, he was offending against the righteousness of God. Inhumanity was a *religious* offence. We entirely miss the impact of the first chapter of the book of Amos, in which the prophet castigates the nations for their crimes against common humanity (and not, as we might expect, against Israel), unless we appreciate that such conduct is declared to be *an act of rebellion against the God of Israel*:

> Thus says the LORD:
> 'For three transgressions of the Ammonites,
>   and for four, I will not revoke the
>   punishment;
> because they have ripped up women with child
>   in Gilead,
>   that they might enlarge their border.'
>
> Thus says the LORD:
> 'For three transgressions of Moab,
>   and for four, I will not revoke the
>   punishment;

1. I Sam. 14. 24–45; II Sam. 6. 6–7; 24. 1–25; Lev. 4; 5. 1–4; 22. 14.

because he burned to lime
the bones of the king of Edom.'¹

There is no question here of a breach of a code of law, as the
translation 'transgression' may suggest. The Hebrew word
pésha‘ means rebellion against a person.² What the prophet
said, therefore, was 'for three acts of *rebellion* (against God),
God will not turn back the devastating doom'. Cruelty, wherever it was to be found, was a defiant spurning of man's distinctively human privilege of 'walking with God'.³

The sins of God's own people were most properly called
acts of rebellion, because they were like a son's unnatural
defiance of his father:

> Hear, O heavens, and give ear, O earth;
> for the LORD has spoken:
> 'Sons have I reared and brought up,
> but they have rebelled against me.'⁴

> But this people has a stubborn and rebellious
> heart;
> they have turned aside and gone away.⁵

Sin for the prophets, therefore, was no mere slip in ritual,
nor an unwitting act to which a capricious deity took exception. It was high-handed⁶ rebellion, deliberate, inhuman,
and treacherous. So said Jeremiah:

> Surely, as a faithless wife leaves her
> husband,
> so have you been faithless to me,
> O house of Israel,
> says the LORD.⁷

For Jeremiah, sinning and forsaking are synonymous terms,
because sin against God is always a personal offence against
love, like an act of adultery.⁸

1. Amos 1. 13; 2. 1.   2. II Kings 3. 5; I Kings 12. 19.
3. Gen. 5. 22, 24; 6. 9; Mic. 6. 8; Mal. 2. 6.   4. Isa. 1. 2.
5. Jer. 5. 23; cf. Deut. 21. 18; Jer. 2. 29; 3. 13; Hos. 7. 13; Zeph. 3. 11.
6. See Num. 15. 30.   7. Jer. 3. 20.
8. Jer. 1. 16; 3. 6–10; 9. 2; 23. 10; cf. Hos. 5. 7.

Apart from using expressions of a quasi-technical character, the prophets ransacked their experience and their vocabulary to bring home to Israel the meaning of her wickedness. In the language of the housewife, she was filthy and needed God's cleansing;[1] in the language of the surgeon, she was desperately wounded and needed God's healing hand;[2] in the language of the shepherd, she was a lost sheep, whom God must lead back to the fold;[3] in the language of the farmer, she was grain choked with rubbish;[4] in the language of the metal-worker, she was full of dross and needed God to smelt her;[5] in the language of the builder, she invited demolition;[6] in the language of the slave market, she had sold herself and awaited redemption by her next-of-kin.[7]

These homely terms leave us in no doubt that the intimacy between God and Israel was not regarded by the prophets as an intimacy between equals. It was the privileged relationship of an erring son to a father, whose authority (as the modern world is in danger of forgetting) was beyond dispute.[8] The norm, that is to say, the 'righteousness', of Israel's family life was the absolute righteousness of its head and for this, human experience provided no more than a hint. We noticed earlier how the prophets were conscious of the inadequacy of all human language for describing the God whom they were called to obey and yet how characteristically and superbly his sovereignty is disclosed in their vivid and concrete analogies. In their appeal to human experience and in their recognition of its limitations, they anticipate the teaching of Jesus:

If you then, who are evil, know how to give good gifts to your children, how much more will your Father who is in heaven give good things to those who ask him?[9]

The *how much more* of this saying is not only the ladder set between earth and heaven; it is also the measure of the difference between God and man.

For the great prophets, this difference between God and man was one which could be expressed only in personal and

1. Jer. 2. 22.   2. Isa. 1. 5–6.   3. Jer. 23. 3.
4. Amos 9. 9.   5. Ezek. 22. 18–22.   6. Amos 7. 8.
7. Isa. 50. 1.   8. Jer. 7. 23; Hos. 9. 17.   9. Matthew 7. 11.

moral terms. If they had believed that God was *essentially* different from man, they could easily have said so. The ancient idea of holiness was close at hand. Fundamentally, 'holy' meant cut off from common use, different in kind, distinctively 'divine'.[1] The plain fact, as you may see by glancing at a concordance, is that, generally speaking, the great prophets were not interested in the term. Amos, for example, uses it twice only, as a synonym for 'God in his own nature'.[2] It is the book of Isaiah which stands out as the significant exception. As far as our records allow us to judge, he was the first to describe God as 'the Holy One of Israel' and this title dominates his oracles.[3] It seems probable, however, that Isaiah's understanding of God's holiness is new and distinctive. In his inaugural vision in the Temple, a glowing cloud of smoke from the altar of incense may, perhaps, have suggested to him the radiant presence of God:

> Holy, holy, holy is the LORD of hosts;
> the whole earth is full of his glory.[4]

The prophet did not recoil from his vision with shuddering awe, as if he had become aware of that which was unintelligible and 'wholly other' – the *mysterium tremendum*. On the contrary, his response was personal and moral; he confessed his sin and offered his life in the Lord's service. God had disclosed his majesty and righteousness in a way which he could understand and which he interpreted as a call to the prophetic ministry. When Isaiah spoke of the 'Holy One of Israel', it is legitimate to suppose, therefore, that he was thinking more in terms of God's luminous presence than of any kind of numinous transcendence.[5]

When we use the term 'holy', we ought to be sure that we mean by it no less than Isaiah and his anonymous disciple. In the work of Second Isaiah, the majesty of the Holy One is

1. 1 Sam. 21. 4; Ezek. 22. 26; 42. 20; 44. 23; Exod. 29. 31–4.
2. Amos 4. 2 (cf. 6. 8); 2. 7.
3. Isa. 1. 4; 5. 19, 24; 12. 6; 17. 7, etc.
4. Isa. 6. 3; cf. 1 Kings 8. 10–11; Lev. 16. 12–13. The 'glory' of the Lord often means his radiant presence: Exod. 24. 16; Isa. 4. 4–6; 58. 8; 60. 1–3; Ezek. 1. 28; 10. 4; Hab. 2. 14.
5. Isa. 10. 17; cf. 2. 10, 19, 21.

counterbalanced by a marked emphasis on his intimacy – the intimacy of one who is Israel's kinsman: 'the Holy One of Israel is your Redeemer.'[1] This is holiness with a difference – the difference effected by God's self-revelation. Holiness is no longer a potent 'supernatural something', but the personal character of God himself:

> The LORD of hosts is exalted in justice,
>> and the Holy God shows himself holy in righteousness.[2]

The kind of response which the Holy God demands was given classical expression in the book of Micah:

> He has showed you, O man, what is good;
>> and what does the LORD require of you
> but to do justice, and to love kindness,
>> and to walk humbly with your God?[3]

The writer of these words possessed a profound insight into the character of the God who has now spoken to us by a Son and he has much to teach modern Christendom concerning religion and righteousness.

1. Isa. 54. 5; cf. 41. 14; 43. 3; 47. 4; 49. 7 and pp. 103f.
2. Isa. 5. 16.   3. Mic. 6. 8; cf. Ps. 15.

CHAPTER FIVE

FAITH AND FULFILMENT

A VISITOR to the Sistine Chapel in the Vatican might gather from the celebrated ceiling of Michelangelo that the Hebrew prophets were men whose eyes were always scanning the distant horizons of the future. His frescoes between the side pillars offer alternating studies of the prophets and the sibyls. Between Jeremiah and Ezekiel, as a visitor's guide-book will inform him, is the Sibyl of Persia. The underlying assumption of this art of the early sixteenth century is that Old Testament prophets and pagan soothsayers equally predicted the coming of Christ.

The interpretation of Hebrew prophecy in terms of the prediction of Christ's coming is a misleading method of presenting in popular form one of Christianity's basic beliefs. The conviction that Christ fulfilled 'the things which God foreshowed by the mouth of all the prophets'[1] is evident from the fact that nearly every page of the New Testament is studded with Old Testament quotations and allusions. When these references are carefully examined, it becomes clear that underlying the characteristic choice of Old Testament passages made by such individual writers as Paul and John, there is a solid core of material (notably from Isaiah, Jeremiah, and the Psalms) which most of the New Testament writers use in common.

This significant measure of agreement strongly suggests that at the very beginning the Church had a common mind about the way in which Christians should interpret the Old Testament and about the selection of passages most relevant to the new facts of the gospel. What the first Christians did do and what they did *not* do are equally illuminating for our understanding of Hebrew prophecy.

1. Acts 3. 18; cf. 8. 26-38.

Faith and Fulfilment

PROPHECY AND HISTORY

With rare exceptions,[1] the very first Christian students of the Old Testament did *not* treat the prophets as clairvoyants who forecast the coming of Jesus and the details of his life. It was certainly not on their authority that Michelangelo placed Jeremiah alongside the pagan sibyl. However, the so-called 'argument from prophecy', which seeks to authenticate the revelation of the New Testament by demonstrating that there is a correspondence between prophetic prediction and Christian event, was devised early in the Church's life and is slow to die.

It seemed that this *Old Moore's Almanack* theory of the prophet's function had been dealt a fatal blow when modern students coined the memorable distinction between *fore*tellers and *forth*tellers. But this formula is now often rejected as facile. It is, nevertheless, saying something which cannot be lightly dismissed. The Old Testament world was hag-ridden by foretellers and from these the prophets are sharply differentiated. Prediction, especially in Babylon, was an elaborate 'science' for which there was an elaborate training; in comparison, our Sunday-newspaper astrologers stand exposed as mere silly amateurs. Those who hanker after prediction should study it in its most highly-organized Babylonian form; they would then see the kind of nonsense to which it leads. The Old Testament writers were under no illusions about it and regarded 'any one who practices divination, a soothsayer, or an augur' as a fraudulent menace and the great prophets lavished on all such some of their very best vituperation.[2] Thus they distinguished themselves from the professional prophets, who made clairvoyance part of their stock-in-trade.[3] Apart, however, from their explicit condemnations, it is abundantly clear from the preaching of the prophets that they did not believe that the future was determined in the immutable way which prediction necessarily demands. Their messages of imminent

1. E.g. Matthew 21. 4–7; Zech. 9. 9.
2. Deut. 18. 10; see pp. 40f.
3. 1 Sam. 2. 34 (cf. 4. 11); 3. 19; 9. 5–9; II Sam. 12. 14; I Kings 14. 12; 21. 19 (cf. 22. 38).

doom are explicitly intended to confront Israel with the challenge of the living God at work in the events of history; their purpose is not to predict the future but to shape it, in eliciting the people's loyal response:

> Seek good, and not evil,
> that you may live;
> and so the LORD, the God of hosts,
> will be with you,
> as you have said.
> Hate evil, and love good,
> and establish justice in the gate;
> *it may be* that the LORD, the God of hosts,
> will be gracious to the remnant of Joseph.[1]

The crucial phrase 'it may be' (which would have lost any professional prophet his job) introduces an exposition of the *raison d'être* of Jeremiah's prophecies of doom:

> *It may be* that the house of Judah will hear all the evil which I intend to do to them, so that every one may turn from his evil way, and that I may forgive their iniquity and their sin.[2]

What we learn from such explicit statements and the whole drift of the prophets' preaching is confirmed by what we know of the nature of their personal vocation. Even if detailed prediction were theoretically possible, it would be devoid of any spiritual significance and it would in no sense derive from prophetic *knowledge*, that is, from the prophets' personal intercourse with the God who had called them.[3]

All this, however, is not to deny that the great prophets were very much concerned with coming events and the weakness of the popular formula, which substitutes 'forthtellers' for 'foretellers,' is that it fails to do justice to this fact – fails, that is to say, to give proper weight to the prophets' understanding of history. The clue to the nature of this understanding is, however, not so much foresight as insight – insight which penetrated the political surface of contemporary events and found within them the 'righteous acts of God',[4] the outcropping in history of his purposeful government of the world.

1. Amos 5. 14–15; cf. Jonah 3. 1–10; see, further, p. 70 n. 2.
2. Jer. 36. 3.   3. See pp. 65f.   4. See p. 118.

Superficially, the prophets' conviction that the God of Israel controlled the historical destiny of Israel resembles the belief held in other national religions. Thus Isaiah's affirmation that God had raised up Assyria as 'the rod of his anger' to give Israel the beating she deserved, or (to change the figure) that he had hired Israel's enemy as a man borrows a razor – to shave his people bare (a terrible humiliation for the bearded Hebrew)[1] is not different in superficial *form* from the outlook illustrated, for example, by the famous inscription erected by Mesha, king of Moab, in the ninth century B.C.:

I am Mesha, son of Chemosh ... king of Moab ... Omri, king of Israel ... oppressed Moab many days, because Chemosh was angry with his land ... Now Omri annexed all the land of Madeba, and Israel occupied it ... and Chemosh restored it in many days.[2]

Here, a Moabite king implies that Chemosh, his god, used Omri as the rod of his anger, exactly as Isaiah spoke of God's use of Assyria. Similarly, the conquest of Babylon by Cyrus in 539 B.C. is described in the Cyrus Cylinder as the work of the Babylonian god Marduk:

Marduk ... sought a righteous prince, after his own heart, whom he took by the hand. Cyrus, king of Anshan, he called by name, to lordship over the whole world he appointed him. ... To his city Babylon he caused him to go ... going as a friend and companion at his side. ... Without battle and conflict he permitted him to enter Babylon. He spared his city Babylon a calamity.

Again, in *form*, this religious interpretation of Cyrus' conquest is closely parallel to the affirmation of Second Isaiah that Cyrus, in conquering Babylon, was called and led by the *God of Israel* to forward his purpose.[3] These similarities make it clear that the significance of the prophets' 'interpretation of history' lies deeper than their ascription of this and that contemporary event to the activity of their God. One need not go into the question very deeply to appreciate that the attribution of isolated events to the will of God may easily become a glib and hollow convention. In the historical books

1. Isa. 10. 5; 7. 20; cf. Jer. 25. 9; 27. 6; 43. 10.
2. Cf. II Kings 3. 4–27, especially v. 18.
3. Isa. 45. 1; 44. 28; 46. 11.

of the Old Testament and in some of the popular stories of the Pentateuch, for instance, it is difficult to avoid the impression that the writers found it all too easy to affirm that whatever foreign nations did was simply the manifestation of the working of Israel's national God.[1]

The uniqueness of the great prophets' understanding of history derives, then, not from the fact that it was 'religious', but from the fact that it was part of a *unique* religion – a religion which was historical by origin and intrinsic character. The historical fortunes of Israel confronted her with the righteousness of the God who had called her to be his loyal servant at the Exodus deliverance. Religion was not a way of making sense of history; history, rather, was a meeting point – the point at which God ceaselessly called Israel to discern and pursue the righteous purpose of which she was designed to be the embodiment. When other nations were content to believe that history went round in circles, the Mosaic faith was proclaiming that the God who had called Israel into being was directing world events towards a final goal. History was meaningful, because it was getting somewhere; it was getting somewhere, because it was being taken somewhere; it was in the hands of God, the living Creator and Governor of the world.

This conviction is fundamental to Israel's prophetic faith, as it finds expression both in the individual books of the Old Testament and in the whole story of Israel which the books combine to present. The Hebrew scriptures proclaim a revelation in *events*. The poems of Second Isaiah, better than any single book of the Old Testament, disclose the pattern of Israel's historic faith. The Creator of the world is no cosmic clock-maker who, having made the universe, left it to tick over alone. The world's Creator is none other than the God who called Israel to be his servant and witness.[2] Her punishment in exile[3] and her imminent restoration[4] are equally his righteous acts; Babylon's conquest of Jerusalem[5] and Cyrus'

---

1. Judg. 2. 20–2; 3. 2–4; Gen. 41. 38–45; II Chron. 2. 11; 35. 20–1; Ezra 1. 1–4.

2. Isa. 40. 12–31; 41. 8–10; 42. 5–9; 43. 10.

3. Isa. 40. 2.   4. Isa. 51. 1–16.   5. Isa. 42. 23–4.

conquest of Babylon[1] both belong to his ongoing purpose. That purpose embraces the whole world, achieving in universal redemption the ultimate goal towards which the initial act of creation was the first step.[2] Between Creation and Redemption lies History – the history of Israel amid the nations of the world – and in all three spheres God manifests his unique sovereignty.[3] Only the eternal God,[4] the first and the last, knows the beginning, the course, and the end of world history.[5]

God knows the inner workings of history, because he controls them; and what he knows he is able to reveal. The revelation made to Second Isaiah in the divine council[6] is the good news – the gospel – of Israel's imminent restoration; God is about to perform a new thing.[7] The prophet's preoccupation with the immediate future and its bearing on the present situation is akin to that of his predecessors, but in some respects his outlook on the future is without parallel. The salvation he announces is determined; although it is of the most momentous relevance to the present situation, it does not arise out of it. The emphasis falls on the decision and action of God rather than on his people's response. This explains why the prophet describes God's superiority to the idols of Babylon as consisting in his ability to *foretell the future*:

> I am God, and there is none like me,
>   declaring the end from the beginning
>   and from ancient times things not yet done,
>   saying, 'My counsel shall stand,
>   and I will accomplish all my purpose.'[8]

Although prediction undeniably enters Second Isaiah's conception of God's prophetic revelation, he himself never indulges in remote prognostication. The characteristic contribution of prophecy to knowledge of the future is not the revelation of any detailed sequence of events (which is *never* to be found),

1. Isa. 44. 24–45. 13.
2. Isa. 45. 20–3; 51. 4–5.
3. Isa. 45. 9–13.
4. Isa. 40. 28.
5. Isa. 44. 6–8; 45. 18–19; 46. 8–11.
6. Isa. 40. 1–2; see, further, pp. 45f.
7. Isa. 43. 18–19.
8. Isa. 46. 9–10; cf. 41. 21–9; 42. 8–9; 43. 9; 44. 6–8; 45. 20–1; 48. 3–8, 16.

but the insight which sees the master-plan of the living and purposeful God within the complexity of events. The prophets teach us to recognize in history God's acts of judgement and redemption – in the history of Israel, in the history of our own times, and, above all, in the history of which the New Testament is the record and to which it is the response. It is the master-plan of the Creator which the prophets saw – 'My counsel shall stand, and I will accomplish all my purpose' – and which the first Christians declared had been actualized in the life, death, and resurrection of Jesus Christ.

THE BLESSINGS OF THE KINGDOM

Before we can fully understand how the prophetic faith of Israel took shape as a hope which looked towards its fulfilment in Christ, it is necessary to grasp the fact that the Hebrews set a very high value on life in this present world. Their natural centre of gravity was the present and not the future, this world and not the world to come. The last thing of which they could be accused is pietistic escapism.

The most telling evidence of the Israelites' attachment to this world is to be found in their conception of the monarchy. Once the tribes had settled down in Canaan, it was perhaps inevitable that they should have demanded a king: 'Now appoint for us a king to govern us *like all the nations.*'[1] Their political and commercial ambitions impelled them to follow the way of the world, and the prophets' deep-rooted suspicion of the monarchy[2] reveals the permanent tension which existed between the people's original nomadic faith and the religion and morals of the kingdom. Nevertheless, from the moment of its inception, the monarchy in Israel was an explicitly religious institution and the modifications which it underwent when it was taken over from the Canaanites show how decisively the Mosaic faith had made itself felt. Now it was the king who upheld and embodied God's covenant with Israel. The royal version of the covenant was, it is true, a revised version of the Exodus tradition, but it remained, nevertheless, emphatically Israelite.

1. 1 Sam. 8. 5.　　　　　2. See p. 75.

Although the unique sovereignty which Israelite faith recognized as belonging to God alone excluded the common oriental notion that the king was identical with God, he was regarded, nevertheless, as superhuman and the 'son of God' by adoption.[1] He was chosen by God for his high office[2] and the divine choice was sealed in an elaborate ceremony of anointing, coronation, and enthronement.[3] The British Coronation Rite stands in a tradition which has changed remarkably little for three thousand years. The most important part of the ritual was the priestly anointing; it was by this that the heir to the throne actually became king – set apart, sacrosanct, and endowed with the spirit of God.[4] In a supreme sense, the king was God's 'servant'.[5] Through him, it was believed, the blessing of God flowed out to the community; on his strength and integrity, the welfare and peace of the whole people was thought to depend.[6] Under God, the anointed king was the keystone of civilized existence and guarantor of all that the Hebrew understood by 'wholeness' of life. In the vivid phrase of an exilic writer, the Lord's Anointed was the breath of the people's nostrils.[7] This deep-rooted and far-reaching conviction is magnificently expressed in one of the 'royal' psalms, which may well have been written for a coronation:

May the King uphold God's covenant

Give the king thy justice, O God,
    and thy righteousness to the royal son!
May he judge thy people with righteousness,
    and thy poor with justice!
Let the mountains bear prosperity for the people,
    and the hills, in righteousness!
May he defend the cause of the poor of the people,
    give deliverance to the needy,
    and crush the oppressor!

May he live while the sun endures,
    and as long as the moon, throughout all generations!

1. Pss. 2. 7; 45. 6; 110. 1; Jer. 22. 18; 34. 5; II Sam. 7. 14; 14. 17.
2. Ps. 89. 19; II Sam. 7. 8.
3. I Kings 1. 32–53; II Kings 11. 9–12.
4. I Sam. 10. 1–6; 26. 9; II Sam. 1. 14–16; cf. Isa. 11. 2.
5. I Kings 3. 7–9; Ps. 89. 3, 20.
6. Pss. 132. 11–18; 20. 6–9.   7. Lam. 4. 20.

May he be like rain that falls on the mown grass,
    like showers that water the earth!
In his days may righteousness flourish,
    and peace abound, till the moon be no more!

May the King enjoy world sovereignty

May he have dominion from sea to sea,
    and from the River to the ends of the earth!
May his foes bow down before him,
    and his enemies lick the dust!
May the kings of Tarshish and of the isles
    render him tribute,
may the kings of Sheba and Seba bring gifts!
May all kings fall down before him,
    all nations serve him!

May the King and his land prosper

Long may he live,
    may gold of Sheba be given to him!
May prayer be made for him continually,
    and blessings invoked for him all the day!
May there be abundance of grain in the land;
    on the tops of the mountains may it wave;
    may its fruit be like Lebanon;
and may men blossom forth from the cities
    like the grass of the field!
May his name endure for ever,
    his fame continue as long as the sun!
May men bless themselves by him,
    all nations call him blessed![1]

This splendid prayer reveals the king at the centre of a religion which was both strongly prophetic and unashamedly worldly in its conception of blessing. Before the disruption of the kingdom of Judah in 586 B.C., expectation turned not towards the future, but towards the royal line of David.

What the ordinary Israelite looked for in life was God's blessing – in peace on earth among men of goodwill. There is a story in Isaiah of an Assyrian officer, who tried to undermine the morale of Jerusalem in the siege of 701 B.C., by offering its citizens a New Order. The terms in which he described it shows him to have been a most excellent propagandist:

1. Ps. 72. 1–7, 8–11, 15–17.

Do not listen to Hezekiah; for thus says the king of Assyria: Make your peace with me and come out to me; then every one of you will eat of his own vine, and every one of his own fig tree, and every one of you drink the water of his own cistern; until I come and take you away to a land like your own land, a land of grain and wine, a land of bread and vineyards.[1]

Similarly blissful pictures of 'three acres and a cow' for every man in a world at peace became a regular feature of the prophetic writings after the fall of Jerusalem. They express the exiles' faith in the restoration of the blessings of the kingdom:

> they shall sit every man under his vine
> and under his fig tree,
> and none shall make them afraid;
> for the mouth of the LORD of hosts has spoken.[2]

Thus says the LORD of hosts: Old men and old women shall again sit in the streets of Jerusalem, each with staff in hand for very age. And the streets of the city shall be full of boys and girls playing in its streets.[3]

Living to a ripe old age was a sure indication of God's blessing. This feature of the ordinary Israelite's ideal of happiness occurs at the end of a passage in Job, which well sums up the Old Testament's attachment to *this* world:

> Behold, happy is the man whom God reproves;
> therefore despise not the chastening of
> the Almighty ...
> For you shall be in league with the stones of the field,
> and the beasts of the field shall be at
> peace with you.
> You shall know that your tent is safe,
> and you shall inspect your fold and
> miss nothing.
> You shall know also that your descendants shall
> be many
> and your offspring as the grass of the earth.
> You shall come to your grave in ripe old age,
> as a shock of grain comes up to the
> threshing floor in its season.[4]

1. Isa. 36. 16–17.   2. Mic. 4. 4; cf. 1 Kings 4. 25.
3. Zech. 8. 4–5.
4. Job 5. 17, 23–6; cf. Prov. 3. 2, 16; 10. 27; Isa. 65. 20–2; Exod. 20. 12; Gen. 24. 60; 26. 12–14.

The Hebrews set great store by the possession of a large family, especially of sons, who would preserve the family name. The desire to live on in one's family is the Jewish version of the Greeks' longing for immortality. It accounts for what may seem to us the curious law of Levirate marriage, whereby it was the duty of a man whose brother died childless to take his widow as his wife and raise children by her, 'that his [brother's] name may not be blotted out of Israel'.[1] This high regard for the life of the family was one of the secrets of the Hebrews' moral strength and stability; it has much to teach the modern world.

Security, wealth, and children make up what may seem a strangely materialistic view of human well-being, even when it was lived out in the faith and fear of God. But is it any more strange than the doctrine, held by some Christian thinkers, that this world is a vale of tears, in which we make preparation for the welfare of our souls in the world to come? Is there anything more intrinsically spiritual in our looking forward to 'Jerusalem the golden, with milk and honey blest', than in our joyful and grateful appreciation of the blessings of God in *this* world? It can at least be said for the Hebrew view that, in relating the material world to the beneficence of God, it won for it a reverence which is so obviously lacking in our own day. The Old Testament's attachment to *this* world did something towards ensuring (like Christian marriage) that 'the natural instincts and affections, implanted by God, should be hallowed and directed aright'. If this sanctification of the world of the senses is demanded of the Christian,[2] for the Hebrew it was a necessity. He served God and received his blessings in this world or not at all. He simply did not believe that he had a 'soul' which could be saved from this world and receive blessing in the world to come.[3] When he came to his grave in a ripe old age, 'as a shock of grain comes up to the threshing floor in its season', that was the end. The stark contrast between this outlook and the ceaseless quest for immortality in

1. Deut. 25. 5–10; cf. Mark 12. 18–23.
2. 1 Corinthians 6. 19.
3. The phrase in Gen. 2. 7 should not be translated a 'living soul', but a 'living *being*'.

popular religion (through the ages to our own day) is a profit-able and sobering theme for reflection.

The Hebrew thought of himself not as an incarnate 'soul', but as an animated body. The distinction is a vital one, for it meant that he had no being apart from his body, and, there-fore, all his values were expressed in terms of life as he knew it in the body on this earth. The vital distinction for him was not (as for some Christian thinkers influenced by Greek thought) that between the 'spiritual' and the 'material' but that between vitality and weakness. A 'spiritual' man was a 'man of spirit,' full of life, vitalized by the power of God, and not a man who was etherealized and disdainful of the world of the senses.[1] This characteristic view of human nature is the foundation of the Old Testament's realistic concern with practical affairs and the ordinary facts of human experience. It also makes its contribution to the prophets' wonderful grasp of the absolute priority of the personal and moral in religion. It was impossible for a Hebrew to suppose that you could 'save' a man's soul while neglecting to enrich his earthly life. Whenever the Christian Church has borrowed from the Greek world the entirely different view that man is essen-tially a soul trapped and entombed in a body (like a bird in a cage), the Hebrew harmony between matter and spirit and morality and religion has been lost. And the consequences have always been disastrous. Christian thinkers have some-times also borrowed from the Greek world the idea that the 'soul' is immortal by its very nature. Again, difficulties have followed. Only by a series of elaborate speculations has it been possible to reconcile this view with the requirements of He-brew-Christian faith that a man's true life is to be found in fellowship with the living God. The prophets were innocent of the Greek dichotomy between soul and body and of the problems which it raises for personal religion. In common with other Old Testament writers, they did not believe in any significant kind of life after death.

There are only two passages in the Old Testament which unambiguously express faith in a future life. They both come

1. Judg. 3. 10; 11. 29; 13. 25; 14. 6, 19; 1 Sam. 11. 6–7; 16. 13; cf. 1 Kings 10. 5.

from a late period (probably the third and second centuries
B.C.) and neither had any general influence on Old Testament faith. The first comes in a section attached to the book
of Isaiah:

> Thy dead shall live, their bodies shall rise.
> > O dwellers in the dust, wake and sing for joy!
> For thy dew is a dew of light,
> > and on the land of the shades thou wilt let it fall.[1]

The second comes from the last chapter of the book of Daniel
and looks for the resurrection of the very good and the very
bad:

> And many of those who sleep in the dust of the earth shall awake,
> some to everlasting life, and some to shame and everlasting con-
> tempt.[2]

These passages, we notice, contemplate the *resurrection of
the body* to this earth. It was thought that only on this earth
and only in the body was it possible for man to receive either
the blessing or the judgement of God. A return to this earth
after death involved resurrection, because at death the *body*
descended to a subterranean world called Sheol. Thus, for
example, Job faces the prospect of death:

> Are not the days of my life few?
> > Let me alone, that I may find a
> > > little comfort
> before I go whence I shall not return,
> > to the land of gloom and deep darkness,
> the land of gloom and chaos,
> > where light is as darkness.[3]

The underworld of Sheol is the opposite of all that is meant
by light and life, a region of near-annihilation[4] and forgetful-
ness, which devours men like a monster and locks them within
its gates without possibility of escape.[5] Its dead inhabitants

1. Isa. 26. 19.   2. Dan. 12. 2.
3. Job 10. 20–2; cf. 30. 23; Isa. 28. 15, 18; Hab. 2. 5; Num. 16. 30–4;
Jonah 2. 1–6.
4. The underworld is also called 'Abaddon' or 'Destruction'; see Job
26. 6; 28. 22; Prov. 15. 11.
5. Ps. 107. 18; Job 7. 9.

are mere shadows,[1] characterized by an appalling weakness, cut off from fellowship with God:

> For in death there is no remembrance of thee;
>   in Sheol who can give thee praise?[2]

The assumption (it was hardly a conviction) that at death man is like water which has been spilt on the ground led the calculating and disillusioned Ecclesiastes to advise his readers to make the best of their present opportunities:

> Whatever your hand finds to do, do it with your might; for there is no work or thought or knowledge or wisdom in Sheol, to which you are going.[3]

This writer represents life as a fight against time. The prophets, on the contrary, though they shared Ecclesiastes' assumption about the utter finality of death, never showed any concern about the brevity of life. Their thoughts were otherwise engaged.

Before we apologize for the inadequacy of Hebrew faith in this respect, we ought to remember what profound spiritual insight the prophets attained without a belief in the life everlasting. Undoubtedly, from the Christian point of view, the faith of the prophets is limited, because they never affirmed that God's sovereignty embraced every individual to all eternity, as they came to affirm that it embraced all the nations of the world. The limitation, however, is more formal than real, since it was a limitation less in their knowledge of God, than in their appreciation of the independence of the individual person from the life of the community. As we shall see later, the prophets were convinced that God would not finally suffer his *people* to perish. Israel would be raised up to newness of life and ransomed from exile.[4] We must seek the fullness of prophetic faith in their hope for Israel and not in what they had to say about the destiny of the individual. That is a modern emphasis which the prophets did not share.

1. Isa. 14. 9–11; 26. 14, 19; Job 26. 5; Ps. 88. 10; Prov. 2. 18.
2. Ps. 6. 5; cf. Pss. 28. 1; 30. 9; 88. 10–12; 115. 17; 143. 7; Isa. 38. 18. In Pss. 16. 10; 30. 3; 49. 15; 86. 13, etc., the meaning appears to be 'saved from going down to Sheol' and not 'raised up out of Sheol'.
3. Eccles. 9. 10.   4. Ezek. 37. 1–14; see, further, pp. 141–9.

THE LOSS AND RESTORATION OF THE KINGDOM

The Exile made a faith which embraced the future essential for continuing faith in the present. The deportation in 597 and 586 B.C. of a fair proportion of the leading inhabitants of Judah to Babylon disrupted the social cohesion of the community of Israel and threatened the whole future of the faith which was so closely bound up with its life. It is difficult for us to imagine what the Exile meant for the Jews in terms of personal loss and social upheaval. Family ties and possessions, their highly-treasured sense of security, the Temple and its sacrificial worship, and the whole familiar structure of their monarchical society were all suddenly and ruthlessly torn away. The kingdom of David had been wiped out and the Lord's Anointed humiliated.[1] The Jews became displaced persons and their fatherland the prey of opportunist squatters.

The little-read book of Lamentations supplies contemporary evidence of what the fall of Jerusalem meant to its agonized inhabitants:

> The Lord has destroyed without mercy
>   all the habitations of Jacob;
> in his wrath he has broken down
>   the strongholds of the daughter of Judah;
> he has brought down to the ground in dishonour
>   the kingdom and its rulers.
>
> The Lord has become like an enemy,
>   he has destroyed Israel;
> he has destroyed all its palaces,
>   laid in ruins its strongholds;
> and he has multiplied in the daughter of Judah
>   mourning and lamentation.
>
> He has broken down his booth like that of a garden,
>   laid in ruins the place of his appointed feasts;
> the LORD has brought to an end in Zion
>   appointed feast and sabbath,
> and in his fierce indignation has spurned
>   king and priest.

1. Lam. 4. 20.

All who pass along the way
　　clap their hands at you;
they hiss and wag their heads
　　at the daughter of Jerusalem;
'Is this the city which was called
　　the perfection of beauty,
　　the joy of all the earth?'[1]

As we have seen, Jeremiah had tried to prepare his country
men for the catastrophe. He had warned them that Nebuchadrezzar's invasion was inspired by God as a judgement on
their sins and, when the blow fell, he had given them the
assurance that their defeat could not cut them off from communion with God. The people had been singularly unim-
pressed. If they had heeded his advice, they would have
settled among their conquerors and there would have been
no problem:

Thus says the LORD of hosts, the God of Israel, to all the exiles
whom I have sent into exile from Jerusalem to Babylon: Build houses
and live in them; plant gardens and eat their produce. Take wives
and have sons and daughters; take wives for your sons, and give your
daughters in marriage, that they may bear sons and daughters;
multiply there, and do not decrease. But seek the welfare of the city
where I have sent you into exile, and pray to the LORD on its behalf,
for in its welfare you will find your welfare ... For I know the plans
I have for you, says the LORD, plans for welfare and not for evil, to
give you a future and a hope. Then you will call upon me and come
and pray to me, and I will hear you. You will seek me and find
me; when you seek me with all your heart.[2]

If Jeremiah's view had prevailed, it is difficult to suppose that
there would have been a post-exilic restoration in Jerusalem
quite of the kind which followed the decree of Cyrus in 538
B.C. Those who were its leaders did all they could to emphasize the distinctiveness and separateness of the holy people.

Inevitably, most of the exiles thought of their deportation
to Babylon as an unmitigated disaster. It deprived them of
all that made life worth living and seriously undermined their
superficial belief that Israel had a special purpose in the provi-
dence of God:

1. Lam. 2. 2, 5, 6, 15.　　　　　2. Jer. 29. 4-7, 11-13.

The word of the LORD came to Jeremiah: 'Have you not observed what these people are saying, "The LORD has rejected the two families which he chose"? Thus they have despised my people so that they are no longer a nation in their sight.'[1]

The taunts of the nations must have raised horrible suspicions in many a Jewish heart. The Exile seemed to disprove the former prophets' insistence on Israel's vocation, although, indeed, their warnings of judgement by captivity had been fulfilled up to the hilt.[2] That part of the prophets' teaching had been forgotten. And so the exiles sat down by the waters of Babylon and wept – unable to sing the Lord's song in a strange land. It is more than probable that the religion of the people had not entirely out-grown the primitive belief that lands other than Palestine were unclean and it was impossible for them to revise all in a moment their conviction that God's habitation was in the Temple at Jerusalem. It is not surprising, therefore, that many of the exiles were almost overwhelmed with despair:

Behold, they say, 'Our bones are dried up, and our hope is lost; we are clean cut off.'[3]

Almost overwhelmed, but not quite. Although the faith of the exiles was only rarely deep enough and spiritual enough to enable them to create a new community and a new pattern of religious practice outside Palestine, yet it had enough resilience to enable them to respond to promises of restoration. Such promises make up the bulk of the prophetic literature which remains for us to explore.

There was, as we have seen, an interpretation of the Exile which rose triumphantly above despair no less certainly than it went over the heads of those who heard it. It is that embodied in Second Isaiah's vision of the Suffering Servant.[4] Israel had been swept out of Palestine not only for punishment, but to bear witness to the world in vicarious suffering. The Cross of the Servant, however, was a scandal in the eyes

---

1. Jer. 33. 23–4; cf. Ezek. 18. 25–7; 33. 17; Mic. 7. 10; Joel 2. 17; Ps. 79. 10.
2. E.g. Jer. 16. 10–13; Ezek. 14. 12–23.
3. Ezek. 37. 11.   4. See pp. 87ff.

of the nations and but cold comfort to the common people. They listened gladly only to those teachers who confined their preaching to the privileges of the covenant and prophesied unconditional restoration to their own land. This Cross, therefore, was to remain a light in a world of comparative darkness, until One full of grace and truth came and bore its pains for the world's salvation.

When the way of the Servant, like the advice of Jeremiah, failed to evoke a response, it was fortunate that there were teachers like the prophet whose preaching is preserved in certain chapters (notably 33–39) of the book of Ezekiel. The outlook here is sufficiently akin to that of the people to enable it to speak to their condition:

> Therefore thus says the Lord GOD: Now I will restore the fortunes of Jacob, and have mercy upon the whole house of Israel; and I will be jealous for my holy name. They shall forget their shame, and all the treachery they have practiced against me, when they dwell securely in their land with none to make them afraid, when I have brought them back from the peoples and gathered them from their enemies' lands, and through them have vindicated my holiness in the sight of many nations. Then they shall know that I am the LORD their God because I sent them into exile among the nations, and then gathered them into their own land. I will leave none of them remaining among the nations any more; and I will not hide my face any more from them, when I pour out my Spirit upon the house of Israel, says the Lord GOD.[1]

Although the oracles of the book of Ezekiel are notoriously difficult to date, we may fairly suppose that this passage is not unrepresentative of a certain kind of prophetic teaching in Babylon. Some of Israel's leaders were convinced that all the exiles would be restored to their own land[2] and that peace and prosperity awaited them there.[3] Further, it would seem, the argument was put forward that the prestige of God was too closely bound up with the fortunes of Israel for any different outcome of the disaster which had befallen them. The idea that God's holy name had been profaned by the misdeeds and

1. Ezek. 39. 25–9.
2. Ezek. 16. 53; 11. 17–19; 20. 40–4; 37. 15–23.
3. Ezek. 34. 11–31; 36. 28–38.

misfortunes of Israel[1] and the conviction that her restoration in the sight of the nations was necessary in order that they should recognize God's power and glory[2] are among the dominant themes of the book of Ezekiel. Although a similar awareness is not quite absent from Second Isaiah,[3] it is difficult to avoid the conclusion that it is developed in Ezekiel to a degree which mirrors a mind that was dogmatic and coarse. Israel is thought of, not so much as the object of God's loving care, as a privileged pawn in a grand theological game.[4] Those who are able to find in this teaching a magnificent conception of divine grace (which, there can be no doubt, is *formally* present)[5] may count themselves fortunate. However appreciative we are of the miracle by which Israel was able to retain any sense of vocation at all in Babylon, no useful purpose is served by concealing one's impression that here, as elsewhere in the writings of the period, we have the treasure of the exiles' faith in earthen vessels. The exigencies of the hour sometimes stimulated a type of teaching which seems more like the perils the pre-exilic prophets fought than a genuine development of their insight.

Although recent studies have done much to restore the insecure reputation of the later prophets, the first of Zechariah's visions betrays an unmistakable change of emphasis:

Then the angel of the LORD said, 'O LORD of hosts, how long wilt thou have no mercy on Jerusalem and the cities of Judah, against which thou hast had indignation these seventy years?' And the LORD answered gracious and comforting words to the angel who talked with me. So the angel who talked with me said to me, 'Cry out, Thus says the LORD of hosts: I am exceedingly jealous for Jerusalem and for Zion. And I am very angry with the nations that are at ease; *for while I was angry but a little* they furthered the disaster. Therefore, thus says the LORD, I have returned to Jerusalem with compassion; my house shall be built in it, says the LORD of hosts, and the measuring line shall be stretched out over Jerusalem. Cry again, Thus says the LORD of hosts: My cities shall again overflow

1. Ezek. 36. 20–2; 34. 29; 35. 12; 36. 6, 15; cf. 20. 9.
2. Ezek. 36. 23, 35–6; 39. 27.
3. Isa. 42. 6–8; 45. 6; 55. 5.
4. Ezek. 36. 32; 39. 25; cf. 20. 44.
5. Ezek. 20. 44; 34. 11–16, 25–31; 37. 14.

with prosperity, and the LORD will again comfort Zion and again choose Jerusalem.'[1]

From the telling admission 'for while I was angry *but a little*', we see how the balance of responsibility for the sufferings of the Exile was gradually being shifted from Israel's own rebellion to the vindictiveness of the nations.[2] It is difficult to think that these gracious and comforting words would have won the unqualified support of the great prophets of the pre-exilic period. Characteristically, they fulfilled their vocation, as Jeremiah admitted, when they 'prophesied war, famine, and pestilence against many countries and great kingdoms.'[3] In the name of God, they challenged an order that was established in apostasy and threatened it with destruction. After the collapse of the kingdom, their successors turned their thoughts to restoration and reconstruction. They were charged with the task of building a New Order and that demanded qualities which, candour compels us to confess, are less easily recognized as being 'prophetic'. If it is usually the lot of the prophet to be at logger-heads with his own people, the prophets of the Exile had to be different. Men like Zechariah were certainly different and were conscious that the times in which they lived were separated by a great gulf from the days of 'the former prophets':

But now I will not deal with the remnant of this people as in the former days, says the LORD of hosts.[4]

Zechariah's use of the term 'remnant'[5] here recalls the magnitude of the change which the Exile brought about. Basically, the word 'remnant' means what has been left over after the bulk has been removed – most frequently by violent death or captivity.[6] The contexts in which the Hebrew root is used generally suggest that the residual part is less important

1. Zech. 1. 12–17.
2. Isa. 10. 5–7; Obad. 12; Mic. 7. 8; Ezek. 35. 15.
3. Jer. 28. 8.   4. Zech. 8. 11; cf. 1. 4–5; 7. 7, 12.
5. The following paragraphs are confined to a brief examination of the use of the principal Hebrew root and related nouns. The general 'idea of the remnant' in such passages as Gen. 7. 23; 18. 23–33; 1 Kings 19. 18; Isa. 1. 9 and Ezek. 11. 19–20 is not our present concern.
6. Deut. 4. 27; II Kings 7. 13; 25. 22; Ezra 1. 4.

than that which has been lost.[1] The prophets before the Exile most frequently employ the term in its normal, non-technical meaning; as, for example, Jeremiah, who uses it to describe the residue of the people left in Jerusalem after the Babylonian deportation of 597 B.C.:

> But thus says the LORD: Like the bad figs which are so bad they cannot be eaten, so will I treat Zedekiah the king of Judah, his princes, *the remnant of Jerusalem* who remain in this land, and those who dwell in the land of Egypt. I will make them a horror to all the kingdoms of the earth, to be a reproach, a byword, a taunt, and a curse in all the places where I shall drive them.[2]

Ezekiel, similarly, calls the residue left in Jerusalem a 'remnant', using the term without any special significance or suggestion of hope.[3] But sometimes the pre-exilic prophets deliberately announce that there will be a 'remnant' of the people and then their intention is to give warning of an overwhelming judgement to come. Thus Amos declares:

> For thus says the Lord GOD:
> 'The city that went forth a thousand
>   shall have a hundred *left*,
> and that which went forth a hundred
>   shall have ten *left*
>   to the house of Israel.'[4]

The purpose of this dirge is not to promise the preservation of the hundred or the ten, but to threaten the house of Israel with devastating destruction. The threatening suggestion of the term 'remnant' is the most likely explanation of the cryptic name which Isaiah gave to his son:

> And the LORD said to Isaiah, 'Go forth to meet Ahaz, you and Shear-jashub your son, at the end of the conduit of the upper pool on the highway to the Fuller's Field, and say to him, "Take heed, be quiet, do not fear, and do not let your heart be faint ..."'[5]

The name 'Shear-jashub' may mean either 'a remnant will return' or '*only* a remnant will return', as is clear from

1. Exod. 10. 12, 26; Lev. 5. 9; Josh. 11. 22; II Kings 24. 14.
2. Jer. 24. 8–9; cf. 8. 3.; 15. 9; 21. 7; 38. 4, 22; 40. 6; 42. 15.
3. Ezek. 5. 10; 6. 12; 9. 8; 11. 13; 17. 21.
4. Amos 5. 3; cf. 3. 12; Exod. 22. 13.   5. Isa. 7. 3–4.

two later interpretations in the book of Isaiah. In the first passage, the name is read as a promise that a remnant will return to God in penitence[1] and in the second as a message of doom:

> For though your people Israel be as the sand of the sea, only a remnant of them will return (*she'ār yāshûbh*). Destruction is decreed, overflowing with righteousness.[2]

It is probable that Isaiah named his son to convey a warning on some occasion *before* the crisis which faced Judah when he met Ahaz outside the walls of Jerusalem – the child, after all, appears to have been old enough to walk – and that his presence with his father was a reminder of the disaster which would befall, if the king turned to Assyria instead of to God.

After 586 B.C., when Jerusalem fell and prophetic threat became historical fact, the exiles (not unnaturally) called themselves the 'remnant'. Such were the pathetically puzzled group who came to Jeremiah, saying:

> Let our supplication come before you, and pray to the LORD your God for us, for all this remnant (for we are left but a few of many, as your eyes see us), that the LORD your God may show us the way we should go, and the thing that we should do.[3]

There were those among the exiles, however, who, so far from giving up hope, came to believe that they had been providentially spared. Their confidence found expression in the reinterpretation and development of 'remnant' as a technical term.[4] Now it was used to describe their status – no longer as the 'remnant' left over from a divine judgement which had been deserved – but as the Remnant purposed by God for the maintenance of his covenant promises. The Remnant is the thin Red Line of loyal faith in a wicked world. Thus an exilic passage of Zephaniah expresses the exiles' belief in their destiny in terms of a divine promise:

1. Isa. 10. 20–1.   2. Isa. 10. 22.
3. Jer. 42. 2–3; cf. 40. 11.
4. Although the term has no explicit doctrinal content in the following passages (all of exilic date), it appears in contexts which express confidence in restoration: Isa. 4. 3; 10. 20–1; 11. 11, 16; 28. 5–6; 37. 31; 46. 3–4; Mic. 2. 12–13; 7. 18; Zeph. 2. 7, 9; Jer. 23. 3–4; 31. 7; Zech. 8. 6, 11.

For I will leave in the midst of you
    a people humble and lowly.
They shall seek refuge in the name of the LORD,
    those who are left in Israel;
they shall do no wrong
    and utter no lies,
nor shall there be found in their mouth
    a deceitful tongue.
For they shall pasture and lie down,
    and none shall make them afraid.[1]

Similarly, an anonymous oracle now embodied in the book of
Micah shows how completely 'remnant' had lost its original
threatening significance. It is now associated with a 'strong
nation' and contrasted with the limping and damaged residue:

In that day, says the LORD,
    I will assemble the lame
and gather those who have been driven away,
    and those whom I have afflicted;
and the lame I will make the *remnant*;
    and those who were cast off, a strong nation;
and the LORD will reign over them in Mount Zion
    from this time forth and for evermore.[2]

It is evident that the so-called 'doctrine of the Remnant',
which is often ascribed to Isaiah,[3] arose among the exilic
residue. It expressed their confidence that they were still within God's covenanted purpose and would be restored to Jerusalem. There can be no question of dismissing the assurance
of the exilic community as bogus, since assurance is one of the
genuine fruits of faith. Nevertheless, religious assurance and
complacent optimism are easily confused, and it is hard to
avoid the impression that there is a difference in spiritual
quality between the hard-won confidence of (say) Second
Isaiah and the self-confidence of some of those who boasted
that they were the Remnant.

1. Zeph. 3. 12–13.
2. Mic. 4. 6–7; cf. 5. 7–8; Isa. 37. 32; Jer. 50. 20; cf. Gen. 45. 7.
3. The nearest approach made by Isaiah to this 'doctrine' is his statement in 1. 9 that God had left 'a few survivors' from the Assyrian siege in
701 B.C.

A development from threat to promise, parallel to that of 'remnant', may be traced for the important term, the 'Day of the Lord'. It, too, illustrates the change which overcame prophecy after the fall of Jerusalem. In the eighth century B.C., when we first meet it in Amos, the 'Day of the Lord' was a popular Utopian catchword, meaning the time when God would shower upon Israel the fullness of his favours and really prove to the world that she was his Chosen People. It is unimportant to pause over the much-debated question as to whether the expression originated in the national cult, or whether the word 'day' is simply an idiom for a 'day of decisive action'. What is important is the fact that Amos and the pre-exilic prophets retained the term, but turned its meaning upside down. For them, it no longer meant a gala-day for Israel, but, rather, her day of judgement.[1]

After the fall of Jerusalem, however, there is a distinct shift in emphasis – away from the prophetic reinterpretation of the idea and towards its original popular meaning. Although faithless Jews are still sometimes included in the condemnation, the weight of the Lord's wrath on that day is reserved for the nations and his blessing for Israel:

> For the day of the LORD is near upon all the nations.
> As you have done, it shall be done to you,
> > your deeds shall return on your own head.
>
> But in Mount Zion there shall be those that escape,
> > and it shall be holy;
> and the house of Jacob shall possess their own possessions.[2]

The idea of the 'Day of the Lord' runs through the prophetic books, collecting new shades of meaning as it is used at different times and in different contexts, until, at last, it comes to mean the final victory of God at the end of history, when the divine purpose would reach its consummation. Throughout these developments, it never altogether loses its basic meaning – the Day of the *Lord*, the time when God's sovereignty is manifestly active. *It is the day of which the whole content*

---

1. Amos 5. 18–20; see, further, pp. 69f.
2. Obad. 15, 17; cf. Ezek. 30. 1–5.

is God. Although it is described in fantastic imagery[1] (which is, perhaps, the only language a poet can employ when his subject is the advent of God), it would be a mistake to suppose that the 'Day of the Lord' was a bizarre notion unrelated to the realities of history. Many of the prophets thought of its coming as imminent[2] and the book of Lamentations actually identifies it with the *past* event of Jerusalem's destruction.[3] This combination of earth-shaking language and historical realism is well illustrated in an oracle of Haggai:

> The word of the LORD came a second time to Haggai on the twenty-fourth day of the month, 'Speak to Zerubbabel, governor of Judah, saying, I am about to shake the heavens and the earth, and to overthrow the throne of kingdoms; I am about to destroy the strength of the kingdoms of the nations, and overthrow the chariots and their riders; and the horses and their riders shall go down, everyone by the sword of his fellow. On that day, says the LORD of hosts, I will take you, O Zerubbabel my servant, the son of Shealtiel, says the LORD, and make you like a signet ring; for I have chosen you, says the LORD of hosts.'[4]

Like his contemporary Zechariah,[5] Haggai here is far from turning his back on the concrete situation of the Jews in 520 B.C. and indulging in speculation concerning the imminence of the end of the world. Zerubbabel, the grandson of Jehoiachin and, therefore, of the royal line of David, had been appointed governor of Judah by Darius the Persian king. The accession of Darius to the Persian throne was the signal for widespread revolts throughout his empire. This shaking of the political foundations encouraged Haggai and Zechariah in the belief that God was about to inaugurate his kingly rule in Jerusalem. Zerubbabel, the chosen servant and seal of God,[6] the Branch (or 'Shoot') sprung with new life from the stump of David's family tree,[7] would be anointed and crowned as God's vice-

---

1. Joel 2. 30–1; 3. 15; Nahum 1. 2–11; Isa. 13. 9–10; cf. 1 Kings 19. 11–12.
2. Zeph. 1. 14; Ezek. 30. 3; Joel 1. 15; 2. 1; 3. 14; Isa. 13. 6.
3. Lam. 1. 12; 2. 1; 2. 21–2. 4. Hag. 2. 20–3.
5. Zech. 4. 7; cf. Hag. 2. 6–9.
6. Hag. 2. 23; Zech. 3. 8; cf. Ecclesiasticus 49. 11.
7. Zech. 3. 8; 6. 12.

gerent and Israel's king.[1] Under his rule the Temple would be rebuilt and divine blessing would flow once again in the City of David.[2]

When the eyes of the exilic prophets turned towards the future, they looked in the first place towards a restored Jerusalem.[3] The quality and enduring significance of their vision depend on the degree to which their national and political hopes arise from and are determined by their insight into the character of God. Although, so to speak, it is the excess of their vision over their immediate practical objectives which is most obviously of permanent importance, their policy also has a spiritual motivation and this should not be dismissed as irrelevant to revelation. None of the prophets spoke in a political vacuum. When we get impatient with the limited practical concerns of prophets like Haggai and Zechariah, we do well to recall that the cosmic splendour of Second Isaiah's religious thought is rooted and grounded in his conviction that God was about to restore the exiles to their home in Jerusalem.[4] In this restoration, God's kingly rule would be made manifest. Throughout the prophecy of the exilic and post-exilic periods, these two themes of Israel's restoration and the manifestation of God's sovereignty are inextricably intermingled. What we have to remember is that the two themes *are* inextricable.

As we saw in an earlier chapter, the Old Testament prophets reveal their understanding of God's nature in the accounts they give of Israel's origin as the people of God. Similarly, in their visions of Israel's future destiny, the prophets of this last period reveal – in an even clearer light – their conception of the divine sovereignty. By speaking to their contemporaries of the nature of Israel's vocation, they speak to us of the nature of God's kingly rule. The oracles in which they expressed their faith in the future of their people may, therefore, be read by us as oracles of the Kingdom of God.

1. Zech. 4. 14; 6. 9–15 (Joshua's name has been substituted for that of Zerubbabel in v. 11).
2. Zech. 1. 17; 2. 4–5; 4. 9; 6. 12–13; 8. 4–5; cf. Hag. 2. 2–9, 19.
3. Isa. 58. 12; 60. 10–11; 61. 4; see, further, pp. 23f., 142f., 150ff.
4. See pp. 84–7.

THE ORACLES OF THE KINGDOM

There are more than a hundred oracles in the prophetic books (most of them being anonymous) which affirm the expectation and present a picture of a Good Time Coming, when God would take his power and reign. They form a unity in so far as they all express an unshakable confidence that God would inaugurate his Kingdom on earth and that it would radically transform the chaos and frustration of the writers' times. These oracles differ enormously, however, in their ideas of the form of God's Reign and of the manner in which it would be established. It is essential that we should keep the whole range of these prophetic passages in mind; otherwise, on the evidence of an arbitrary selection, we shall fall into the error of mistaking details for doctrine and of characterizing too narrowly the nature of Israel's hope.

It is not always easy, however, to identify the common ground of prophetic conviction underlying the variety of pre-sentation. For example, the vision of the New Jerusalem in the last nine chapters of the book of Ezekiel is vastly different from the City of David which aroused the enthusiastic ex-pectation of Haggai and Zechariah. The bad record of Judah's kings had not been forgotten by the writer of Ezekiel 40–48, and the prince in his New Jerusalem is little more than a su-perior Minister of Supply, charged with responsibility for the upkeep of the Temple sacrifices.[1] Government is in the hands of the priesthood.[2] The reorganization of the capital is as neat and systematic as any modern town-planner could wish and its express aim is to ensure that the Temple should never again be desecrated by contact with the common life of un-sanctified humanity.[3] Here we have a recrudescence of the primitive notion of holiness as ritual separateness[4] and it was now to find embodiment in bricks and mortar. Ezekiel's town plan carefully screens the Holy Place from the secular life of the city.[5] Details are also laid down for the duties of the priest-

---

1. Ezek. 45. 8–9, 13–17; 46. 16–18.   2. Ezek. 44. 24.
3. Ezek. 42. 20; 43. 7–9; 44. 6–9.
4. Ezek. 42. 14; 44. 19, 23; 46. 20; see, further, p. 122.
5. Ezek. 45. 1–8; 47. 13–48. 35.

hood and the ritual of the sanctuary. The last two chapters of this 'blueprint' give an account of the proposed distribution of the twelve tribes within the boundaries of the land and this is introduced by a description of a phenomenal river which would issue from the Temple and transform desert places into a veritable paradise:

> This water flows toward the eastern region and goes down into the Arabah; and when it enters the stagnant waters of the sea, the water will become fresh. And wherever the river goes every living creature which swarms will live, and there will be very many fish ... And on the banks, on both sides of the river, there will grow all kinds of trees for food. Their leaves will not wither nor their fruit fail, but they will bear fresh fruit every month, because the water for them flows from the sanctuary. Their fruit will be for food, and their leaves for healing.[1]

The unexpected inclusion of the River of Life [2] in Ezekiel's vision of the New Jerusalem is a sharp reminder that the writer is thinking of more than a restoration of the old order. This restoration, though conceived in practical terms, is a re-creation of Paradise. The end in view is nothing less than the consummation of the Creator's original purpose. He will make the last things like the first.[3] That is why the vision ends with the tabernacling of the divine presence with his people: 'And the name of the city henceforth shall be *Yahweh-sham-mah* – The LORD is there.' The new Jerusalem is given a new name for the New Age.[4]

Ezekiel's glorification of Jerusalem and his emphatic proclamation of a theocracy in which God alone is king are among the most characteristic features of exilic and post-exilic prophetic thought. Jerusalem will become the centre of the world,[5] because it is the throne of God [6] and the seat of his universal rule:

1. Ezek. 47. 8–9, 12.
2. Amos 9. 13; Joel 3. 18; Zech. 14. 8; Revelation 22. 1–2.
3. Isa. 51. 3, 9–11; 65. 17; 66. 22; Ezek. 28. 13; 31. 8–9, 16 (cf. Gen. 2); see, further, p. 161.
4. Ezek. 48. 35; cf. 10. 1–22; 11. 22–3; 43. 1–5; Jer. 3. 17; Zech. 8. 3; Isa. 1. 26; 60. 14; 62. 2.
5. Isa. 2. 2–4; 60. 10–11; Mic. 4. 1–4; cf. Ps. 48. 1–3.
6. Jer. 3. 17; 14. 21; 17. 12; Ezek. 43. 7.

for the LORD of hosts will reign
on Mount Zion and in Jerusalem
and before his elders he will manifest
his glory.[1]

All the nations of the earth will come to Zion to pay homage to its King.[2] The universal kingship of God is the fundamental conviction which links together all the prophetic oracles we are considering, and nowhere is it better expressed than in a verse of the last chapter of Zechariah:

And the LORD will become king over all the earth; on that day the LORD will be one and his name one.[3]

This statement is part of a description of the Last Days during which God will annihilate the heathen nations,[4] and it provides the clue to a number of similar passages, which, at first sight, appear not only unspiritual but inexcusably revolting. Joel, for example, contemplates with savage satisfaction the spectacle of the nations gathered together for extermination in 'the valley of decision';[5] and in the prophecy against the legendary King Gog of the land of Magog in Ezekiel, it is calculated that the burial of the slaughtered enemy will occupy no less than seven months.[6] Sentiments of this kind, which are commonly and quite mistakenly supposed to represent the typical thought of the Old Testament, are explicable if not excusable. When the editors of the prophetic books collected the oracles against the nations into great blocks of doom,[7] they were giving expression to their people's bitter experience of persecution. But they were doing more than that. They were also giving expression to their belief that there was a power of evil in the world, which was ranged against the purpose of God and which must be destroyed before his Kingdom could be inaugurated.[8] We do less than justice to these

1. Isa. 24. 23; cf. Zeph. 3. 14–20.
2. Isa. 45. 14; 60. 3; 66. 18–21; Zech. 8. 20–3.
3. Zech. 14. 9 (cf. Deut. 6. 4); cf. Jer. 10. 6–7, 10; Mic. 2. 13; 4. 7; Isa. 33. 22.
4. Zech. 14. 1–5, 12, 15; 12. 9; cf. Zeph. 2. 1–15; Isa. 33. 12; 34. 2.
5. Joel 3. 14.   6. Ezek. 39. 11–14; cf. 39. 17–24.
7. Isa. 13–23; Jer. 46–51; Ezek. 25–32.
8. Isa. 26. 21; Jer. 46. 10–12.

most unattractive oracles, therefore, if we dismiss them as 'mere nationalism'. They are, of course, violently national-istic, but their nationalism is the unworthy vessel in which a valuable cargo is carried. The grievous weakness in their out-look springs from the assumption that the life of Israel was the exclusive sphere in which God's sovereignty could be mani-fested. The important fact about these oracles, however, is not their exclusivism, but the profound conviction they ex-press that God is about to establish his Kingdom and that *his righteous Rule will be undisputed and absolute throughout the world.* Even the unrewarding little book of Obadiah, which hisses threats of annihilation at the Gentiles – 'as you have done, it shall be done to you' – ends with the words: 'and the kingdom shall be the LORD's.'[1]

The universality of God's Reign is by no means always ac-complished in these oracles by the simple expedient of wiping out all the opposition. Some of the prophets were inspired to see a more excellent way. The implication of the belief that God, who had chosen Israel, was the Creator of the world had been grasped by the first of the great editors of Genesis,[2] but it was Second Isaiah who first expressed God's universal sovereignty in terms of a universal faith:

> Turn to me and be saved,
> all the ends of the earth!
> For I am God, and there is no other.[3]

In the New Age to which the prophet looks forward, God not only governs the Gentiles, but asks them to accept his gift of salvation. Israel's vocation is to convey the divine invitation to the whole world and to win it to its true allegiance by vicarious suffering.[4] The vision of Second Isaiah was shared by other anonymous prophets. There are two astonishing oracles at the end of the nineteenth chapter of Isaiah. The first (19. 19–22) looks forward to the conversion of the Egyp-tians; the second (19. 23–25) goes even further:

In that day there will be a highway from Egypt to Assyria, and the Assyrian will come into Egypt, and the Egyptian into Assyria, and

---

1. Obad. 15, 21; cf. Ps. 22. 28; Revelation 11. 15.
2. See pp. 59f.   3. Isa. 45. 22.   4. See pp. 87ff., 140f.

the Egyptians will worship with the Assyrians.

In that day Israel will be the third with Egypt and Assyria, a blessing in the midst of the earth, whom the LORD of hosts has blessed, saying, 'Blessed be Egypt my people, and Assyria the work of my hands, and Israel my heritage.'

This confidence that ancient enemies would be bound together as United Nations without difference or inequality contemplates an extension of the Covenant which is unique in the Old Testament and which foreshadows the New Testament's realization of a People of God in which there is neither Jew or Greek.[1] In the same spirit, other prophets looked upon the new Temple, not as Israel's private chapel for her exclusive communion with God, but rather as 'a house of prayer for all peoples'.[2] And more than one writer affirms that God's sovereignty would be incompletely realized, unless the Gentiles (or at least some of them) shared the salvation of Israel:

> Thus says the Lord GOD
> who gathers the outcasts of Israel,
> I will gather yet others to him
> besides those already gathered.[3]

Many of Israel's spokesmen, however, found it difficult to free themselves from the prejudice that their own people was intrinsically superior to the Gentile nations and to forget that she had suffered humiliation at their hands.[4] In the Day of the Lord, when God made his reckoning with all mankind, they looked forward, therefore, to getting their own back in the subjection of the nations:

The LORD will have compassion on Jacob and will again choose Israel, and will set them in their own land, and aliens will join them and will cleave to the house of Jacob. And the peoples will take them and bring them to their place, and the house of Israel will possess them in the LORD's land as male and female slaves; they will take captive those who were their captors, and rule over those who oppressed them.[5]

1. Colossians 3. 11; 1 Corinthians 12. 13; Romans 10. 12.
2. Isa. 56. 6–7; cf. 45. 23; 60. 1–14; 66. 18–19, 23.
3. Isa. 56. 8; cf. 25. 6–8; see, further, pp. 151f., 155 n. 3.
4. Zeph. 2. 8; Jer. 51. 49; see, further, pp. 140, 152f.
5. Isa. 14. 1–2; cf. 60. 12, 14; 61. 5; Jer. 30. 8, 16; Obad. 15.

It is only too easy for us to condemn this tit-for-tat attitude from the detached security of our arm-chairs and forget that Israel had had to fight for her faith against tremendous odds. Her historical experience inevitably coloured her future expectations, which, we must always remember, were not simply dreams of an ideal order, but hopes of an actual restoration of her life as a community in Palestine.[1]

The remarkable fact is not that the Jews' religious hopes were coloured by political experience, but that her political hopes were basically religious. How difficult it was to avoid nationalistic sentiments is clear from the evidence that no less a prophet than Second Isaiah looked forward in confidence to the time when members of Gentile royal families would become Israel's domestic servants:

> Thus says the Lord GOD:
> 'Behold, I will lift up my hand to the nations,
>   and raise my signal to the peoples;
> and they shall bring your sons in their bosom,
>   and your daughters shall be carried on their
>   shoulders.
> Kings shall be your foster fathers,
>   and their queens your nursing mothers.
> With their faces to the ground they shall bow down to you,
>   and lick the dust of your feet.
> Then you will know that I am the LORD;
>   those who wait for me shall not be put to shame.'[2]

It is clear that in oracles like this there is the conviction that God would one day be King over all the earth, but there is also the suggestion that his Kingdom would not be free from racial discrimination. There is the Master Race on the one hand, and the subject people on the other. Many of the prophets are confident that the Gentiles will come to worship the God of Israel,[3] but some sully their vision by proposing that they will do so under the threat of punishment:

1. Hos. 11. 10–11; Zeph. 3. 19–20; Jer. 30. 3; Ezek. 11. 17; Isa. 48. 20; Zech. 8. 7–8.

2. Isa. 49. 22–3.

3. Zech. 2. 11; 8. 23; Hag. 2. 7; Isa. 56. 3, 6–7; Zeph. 3. 9–10; Jer. 16. 19; cf. Pss. 67; 87; 95–100; and see, further, p. 152.

Then every one that survives of all the nations that have come against Jerusalem shall go up year after year to worship the King, the LORD of hosts, and to keep the feast of booths. And if any of the families of the earth do not go up to Jerusalem to worship the King, the LORD of hosts, there will be no rain upon them. And if the family of Egypt do not go up and present themselves, then upon them shall come the plague with which the LORD afflicts the nations that do not go up to keep the feast of booths. This shall be the punishment to Egypt and the punishment to all the nations that do not go up to keep the feast of booths.[1]

It is almost unnecessary to comment that worship under such compulsion is a fundamental contradiction in terms.

It used to be the fashion to divide the oracles we have been considering into two groups under the labels 'universalist' and 'nationalist'. The assumption was that the former were of permanent significance and that it was legitimate (and even highly desirable) to disregard the latter. This discrimination rests on a comparatively modern insight into the equality of all nations and is, in any case, quite inappropriate as a criterion of Old Testament study. The key simply will not fit the Hebrew lock. There is a vital sense in which the Old Testament is 'nationalistic' from beginning to end, although the term 'particularist' is to be preferred, since it avoids the suggestion that Israel was merely a political entity. The whole of the literature of the Old Testament (except some of the wisdom writings) is concerned with God's self-disclosure in and through his people Israel. We must expect, therefore, that Israelite faith in the ultimate triumph of God's Rule will be expressed in and through the fortunes of Israel. *There is no keeping Israel out of the picture, because she was put there by God.* It follows that the 'particularist' pieces are as important for our understanding of Old Testament revelation as the more attractive 'universalist' passages. No matter how inadequate we find the more popular ideas of Israel's privilege, the prophetic conception of God's election of Israel to a vocation of personal and moral responsibility cannot be discarded. We may even go further and say that if the Mosaic tradition had not explicitly enunciated the belief that Israel had been called

1. Zech. 14. 16–19.

by God, we should ourselves have been forced to formulate a doctrine of Israel's election. The faith of Israel and the witness of the prophets unambiguously demand some such explanation. Israel's election may be (and indeed often was) misunderstood and secularized, but it was known by its fruits. The fullness of prophetic faith outgrows national exclusiveness, but it never outgrows Israel's sense of vocation.

As we have seen, the great pre-exilic prophets' conception of Israel's calling was dominated by the relationship which God inaugurated between his people and himself by the Exodus deliverance.[1] In these later prophetic oracles of the Kingdom there is a marked change in perspective. Although the Exodus deliverance is by no means forgotten and, indeed, is sometimes represented as the 'type' of the New Exodus from Babylon,[2] the emphasis now falls on God's covenant with *David*:

> Incline your ear, and come to me;
> hear, that your soul may live;
> and I will make with you an everlasting covenant,
> my steadfast, sure love for David.[3]

When the exiles looked forward in faith to the inauguration of a new covenant, their hope was that the 'everlasting covenant, ordered in all things and secure',[4] which God had made with David long ago, would once again be the basis of a restored kingdom:

And I will set up over them one shepherd, my servant David, and he shall feed them ... And I, the LORD, will be their God, and my servant David shall be prince among them ... I will make with them a covenant of peace and banish wild beasts from the land, so that they may dwell securely in the wilderness and sleep in the woods. And I will make them and the places round about my hill a blessing; and I will send down the showers in their season; they shall be showers of blessing. And the trees of the field shall yield their fruit, and the earth shall yield its increase, and they shall be secure in their land; and they shall know that I am the LORD.[5]

It would be a mistake to suppose that this covenant with David was wholly different from the covenant with Israel

1. See pp. 56ff. 2. See p. 84 n. 5. 3. Isa. 55. 3.
4. II Sam. 23. 5. 5. Ezek. 34. 23-7.

through Moses. The fact seems to be that the *content* of the Mosaic covenant was given a new form and transferred to David when Israel abandoned her nomadic wanderings in the wilderness, conquered Palestine, and adopted the institution of kingship.[1] Thereafter, it was widely believed (especially in the royal circles of Jerusalem to which Isaiah belonged) that the privileges and responsibilities of being the chosen people of God were received and discharged through the elect and anointed king, whose role, as we have already noticed, was that of a mediator.[2] As the monarchy had played no part in the creative period of Israel's life, and as it was wide open to abuse in the hands of individual kings, tensions between the Davidic and Mosaic traditions inevitably sprang up. In general, the great pre-exilic prophets stand in the Mosaic tradition and are suspicious of the new royal version of the desert covenant.[3] Isaiah of Jerusalem, however, was probably an exception. It is significant that he betrays no interest in the Exodus tradition and (despite the independence of his prophetic ministry) seems at the same time to be deeply attached to the City of David, its Court and its Temple. In every sense, he was a man of Jerusalem and one of its leading and respected citizens.[4] If, as seems probable, Isaiah understood Israel's vocation in terms of the Davidic monarchy, there is no need to argue further that the royal version of the old covenant was far from being incompatible with prophetic faith.

Whatever we may conclude about the status of the monarchy in pre-exilic prophecy, there is no doubt that the dominant hope of prophecy after the fall of Jerusalem was the restoration of the former Davidic kingdom:

> In that day I will raise up
> > the booth of David that is fallen
> and repair its breaches,
> > and raise up its ruins,
> > and rebuild it as in the days of old.[5]

1. II Sam. 7. 8–16; Pss. 18. 50; 89. 1–4, 28–37; 132. 11–12; see, further, p. 130.　　　2. See pp. 131f.　　　3. See pp. 56ff., 130.
4. Isa. 7. 1–17; 8. 2; 9. 1–7; see, further, pp. 77f.
5. Amos 9. 11; cf. Jer. 31. 27–8; Zech. 10. 6; Mic. 4. 8; Isa. 60. 21–2.

The 'days of old' go back to David's undivided kingdom, as is abundantly clear from the constant emphasis on the re-union of Judah and Israel in the coming age.[1] The expectation of these oracles is political and spiritual, historical and theological. The belief is that God will restore the kingdom to Israel, in order to exercise his own universal sovereignty. *The fundamental kingship is always that of God:*

> There is none like thee, O LORD;
>> thou art great, and thy name is great in might.
> Who would not fear thee, O King of the nations?
>> For this is thy due;
> for among all the wise ones of the nations
>> and in all their kingdoms
>> there is none like thee. ...
> But the LORD is the true God;
>> he is the living God and the everlasting King.[2]

Many of the oracles of the kingdom betray no interest in the human agent of God's sovereignty (sometimes, perhaps, because he was taken for granted), but others specify a king of David's line:

Behold, the days are coming, says the LORD, when I will raise up for David a righteous Branch, and he shall reign as king and deal wisely, and shall execute justice and righteousness in the land. In his days Judah will be saved, and Israel will dwell securely. And this is the name by which he will be called: 'The LORD is our righteousness.'[3]

The political form of the faith of these later prophets had clearly not quenched their zeal for righteousness; nor had their historical realism dimmed their vision of the transformation which would take place in the earth when God's Kingdom came. The best summary of the hopes and moral insight which clustered round the coming king is to be found in one of the most familiar and evocative passages of the Old

1. Ezek. 37. 15–22; Jer. 3. 18; 33. 7; Isa. 11. 13; Zech. 10. 6–7.
2. Jer. 10. 6–7, 10; cf. Mic. 5. 4; Obad. 21; Isa. 9. 7; 40. 10; 43. 15; 52. 7; see, further, Isa. 6. 5; 24. 23; 33. 22; Judg. 8. 22–3; 1 Sam. 8. 7; 10. 19; 12. 12.
3. Jer. 23. 5–6; cf. 17. 25; 30. 9; 33. 14–18; Ezek. 34. 23; 37. 24–5; Hos. 3. 5; Mic. 5. 2–4; Isa. 9. 7; 11. 1–9.

Testament – Isa. 11. 1–9. It opens with an announcement of the king's Davidic descent:

> (i) There shall come forth a shoot from the stump of Jesse,
>   and a branch shall grow out of his roots.

The new shoot which would spring from the fallen dynasty of Judah was a regular image in prophetic expectations and probably originated with Zechariah's use of it for Zerubbabel in 520 B.C.[1]

> (ii) And the Spirit of the LORD shall rest upon him,
>   the spirit of wisdom and understanding,
>   the spirit of counsel and might,
>   the spirit of knowledge and the fear of the LORD.

The king is endowed with superhuman powers by God, on whose behalf he bears rule. Although the prophet does not actually describe him as 'the Lord's Anointed',[2] the gift of the Spirit is so closely associated with the rite of anointing[3] that we may take his royal consecration for granted. It is worth pausing to reflect that the Spirit which rests upon God's earthly vicegerent in his Kingdom is none other than the Spirit which some of the prophets (notably Ezekiel and Joel) affirm that God will pour out upon all Israel in the Last Days.[4]

> (iii) He shall not judge by what his eyes see,
>   or decide by what his ears hear;
> (iv) but with righteousness he shall judge the poor,
>   and decide with equity for the meek of the earth;
>   and he shall smite the earth [or, the tyrant] with
>   the rod of his mouth,
>   and with the breath of his lips he shall slay the
>   wicked.
> (v) Righteousness shall be the girdle of his waist,
>   and faithfulness shall be the girdle of his loins.

1. Zech. 3. 8; 6. 12; Jer. 23. 5; 33. 15; Isa. 4. 2.
2. As in the Psalms: 2. 2; 18. 50; 20. 6; 28. 8; 84. 9; 89. 38, 51; 132. 10, 17; see, further, pp. 131, 162.
3. 1 Sam. 10. 1, 6; 16. 13; 11 Sam. 23. 1–2; cf. 1 Kings 19. 16; Isa. 61. 1; Acts 10. 38.
4. Ezek. 36. 27; 37. 14; 39. 29; Joel 2. 28–9; Isa. 32. 15–20; 44.3; Zech 12. 10; cf. Num. 11. 29.

The ruler in God's Kingdom is no arbitrary despot; he is bound by the divine covenant – 'between the LORD and the king and people, that they should be the LORD's people; and also between the king and the people'.[1] The coming king, therefore, will uphold the righteousness of the Lord,[2] which in so many oracles is affirmed to be the pre-condition of a part in the coming Kingdom.[3] The intensely *moral* faith of the prophetic tradition still retains a great deal of its old vigour.

(vi)   The wolf shall dwell with the lamb,
    and the leopard shall lie down with the kid,
and the calf and the lion and the fatling together,
    and a little child shall lead them.

(vii)   The cow and the bear shall feed;
    their young shall lie down together;
    and the lion shall eat straw like the ox.

(viii)   The sucking child shall play over the hole
      of the asp,
    and the weaned child shall put his hand
      on the adder's den.

This idyllic picture of peace and security vividly expresses the consummation of God's purpose. It is, in a word, *Paradise Regained*, that final state of affairs, intended by God (but frustrated by man) from the beginning of the creation. Life in the Kingdom is the enjoyment of peace,[4] health,[5] and prosperity[6] – a new creation shared alike by man, the animals,[7] and the earth.[8] The marvel of it all beggars human language, but the prophets' meaning is clear: *God Reigns*.

1. II Kings 11. 17.
2. Pss. 72. 1–2; 45. 7; see, further, pp. 115–19.
3. Isa. 1. 27–8; 4. 2–6; 32. 15–20; 58. 1–14; 59. 1–21; Ezek. 36. 25; Jer. 33. 8; Zech. 8. 8; Mal. 3. 1–5; Mic. 5. 10–15.
4. Zech. 9. 9–10; Mic. 4. 1–4; 5. 5; Isa. 2. 4; 9. 5, 7; Hos. 2. 18; Jer. 23. 6.
5. Isa. 65. 20–5; 35. 3–6.
6. Amos 9. 13; Isa. 30. 23–5; Ezek. 36. 33–6.
7. The enmity between men and animals announced in Gen. 3. 15 is now abolished: Isa. 65. 25; Hos. 2. 18; Ezek. 34. 25; cf. Lev. 26. 6.
8. See p. 151.

> (ix) They shall not hurt or destroy
> in all my holy mountain;
> for the earth shall be full of the
> knowledge of the LORD
> as the waters cover the sea.

Finally, we are told the inner secret of God's Rule – that 'knowledge' which is nothing less than personal intercourse between man and his Creator and the ground of all blessing.[1] The future king is endowed with 'the spirit of knowledge' and through his mediation Jeremiah's prophecy of the New Covenant will find fulfilment: 'they shall *all* know me, from the least of them to the greatest.'[2]

The coming king of David's line is modelled on the ideal king of pre-exilic Israel and in turn becomes the model for the Messiah of later Judaism. 'The Messiah' (in Greek, 'The Christ') is an expression which never occurs in the Old Testament, although it is derived from the description of Israelite kings as the 'Anointed' (*māshîaḥ*) of the Lord.[3] The Messiah of later Jewish expectation was the Lord's 'Anointed One' *par excellence*, although between the Old and New Testaments many new elements entered into the idea, so that, by the time of the Gospels, he is a heavenly figure and no longer simply the future king who rules for God in his Kingdom on earth. Despite the complicated developments of the period between the two Testaments, however, one of the Messiah's titles – the 'Son of David' – remains as a witness to his royal lineage.[4]

In the light of the evidence we have been considering, the traditional account of the Messianic Hope in the Old Testament and its fulfilment in the New Testament is seen to be inadequate and misleading. Most obviously, we must abandon the type of interpretation (familiar from ecclesiastical art and medieval carols) which finds predictions of Christ's coming in isolated proof-texts.[5] Less obviously, but no less emphatically, we must avoid abstracting the Old Testament 'Messiah'

1. Hos. 6. 2–3; Isa. 43. 10; see, further, pp. 65f.
2. Jer. 31. 34.   3. See p. 131.
4. Mark 10. 47–8; 12. 35–7; Matthew 1. 1; 9. 27; 12. 23; 15. 22; 21. 9, 15; cf. Romans 1. 3; Revelation 3. 7; 5. 5; 22. 16.
5. Gen. 3. 15; 22. 15–18; 49. 10; Num. 24. 17; Isa. 7. 10–14; Pss. 2; 110.

from the Kingdom in which he ruled as God's vicegerent. For the prophets of Israel, it was the Kingdom which brought in the 'Messiah' and not the 'Messiah' who brought in the Kingdom. The 'Messiah' rules in the Kingdom *which God himself has established*. In prophetic faith, the consummation of history is not the Day of the Messiah but the Day of the *Lord*. The sovereignty which the 'Lord's Anointed' is privileged to exercise is the sovereignty of God.

The subordination of the earthly king to the kingly Rule of God which we find in the Old Testament is easily overlooked by Christians, since for them God's kingly Rule, at a particular point in history, was uniquely embodied in a single human Person. It is tempting, therefore, to concentrate exclusively on those parts of the Old Testament which explicitly look forward to the coming of a righteous king. We are now in a better position to recognize how small a proportion of Israel's expectant faith was explicitly concerned with the coming king and, therefore, how much we lose when we thus narrow our interest. Second Isaiah, for example, devotes but a single verse (55. 3) in his sixteen chapters to the royal line of David, and yet, both from the point of view of Old Testament thought and from the point of view of Christian faith, the whole work is of first importance. Even more serious than the passing over of such vital evidence which an exclusively 'messianic' approach to the Old Testament entails is the danger of impoverishing our understanding of the nature of fulfilment in Christ. Christ did not merely fulfil the expectation of a number of prophets that God would raise up a righteous ruler. What he fulfilled was God's disclosure to Israel of his true character and purpose. It was that which enabled the prophets to look forward to the coming of the Kingdom. And it was that which became flesh and dwelt among us, when God reigned in his Son.

THE COMING OF THE KINGDOM

And he came to Nazareth, where he had been brought up; and he went to the synagogue, as his custom was, on the sabbath day. And he stood up to read; and there was given to him the book of the prophet Isaiah. He opened the book and found the place where it was written,

> 'The Spirit of the Lord is upon me,
> because he has anointed me to preach
>   good news to the poor.
> He has sent me to proclaim release to
>   the captives
> and recovering of sight to the blind,
> to set at liberty those who are oppressed,
> to proclaim the acceptable year of the Lord.'

And he closed the book, and gave it back to the attendant, and sat down; and the eyes of all in the synagogue were fixed on him. And he began to say to them, '*Today this scripture has been fulfilled in your hearing.*'[1]

No one category of human thought can embrace the Person of Christ and no one phrase can sum up his work. But of all the paths by which we may approach our Lord, that along which we have been stumbling leads most directly to the secret of his life. If God disclosed himself through the divine-human awareness of the prophets, then to speak of Jesus as *the* Prophet is neither to limit his Godhead, nor to impoverish his Humanity. It is, rather, to substitute for these abstract terms a word which belongs to Jesus' own native tradition and which, in its richest connotation, forbids us to set in opposition the 'human' and the 'divine'.

There is a good deal of evidence to show that Jesus was looked upon by his contemporaries as 'a prophet mighty in deed and word before God and all the people'.[2] His healing of the widow's son at Nain caused a great stir among the crowd, 'and they glorified God, saying, "A great prophet has arisen among us!" and "God has visited his people!" And this report concerning him spread through the whole of Judea and all the surrounding country.'[3] Similarly, the man born blind, when he was healed by Jesus, could only conclude that 'He is a prophet.'[4] It is not surprising, therefore, that the crowds who watched the Triumphal Entry into Jerusalem at

1. Luke 4. 16–21; cf. Isa. 61. 1–2.   2. Luke 24. 19.
3. Luke 7. 16–17; cf. 7. 39.   4. John 9. 17; cf. 4. 19.

the beginning of the last week of Jesus' life, answered the general inquiry, 'Who is this?' by affirming, 'This is the prophet Jesus from Nazareth of Galilee.'[1] And the Pharisees hesitated to arrest him the following day, because the crowds 'held him to be a prophet.'[2] People in general are not much given to precise theological definition, but more than one passage in the gospels indicates the direction in which the minds of ordinary Jews in Jesus' day were tending:

> Now when Jesus came into the district of Caesarea Philippi, he asked his disciples, 'Who do men say that the Son of man is?' And they said, 'Some say John the Baptist, others say Elijah, and others Jeremiah or one of the prophets.'[3]

Peter's epoch-making confession which immediately follows this report of popular opinion reveals its inadequacy and apart from a few other reported references in the Fourth Gospel and the Acts of the Apostles, the New Testament writers do not recognize 'prophet' as a title for Jesus.[4]

More important, however, than the use and non-use of 'prophet' as a title (which, we should bear in mind, depends on the popular understanding of prophecy in the first century A.D.), is the unmistakable evidence that Jesus' vocation is illuminated by that of the great prophets of the Old Testament. Like them, he was conscious that he had been *sent by God:*

> He who receives you receives me, and he who receives me receives him who sent me.[5]

Conversely, the people's rejection of the prophets and Jesus meant no less than their rejection of God.[6] Thus, the Israelites dealt with Samuel:

> And the LORD said unto Samuel, 'Hearken to the voice of the people in all that they say to you: for they have not rejected you, but they have rejected me from being king over them.'[7]

1. Matthew 21. 11. 2. Matthew 21. 46.
3. Matthew 16. 13–14; cf. Mark 6. 15; 8. 28.
4. John 6. 14; 7. 40; Acts 3. 22–3; cf. Deut. 18. 15.
5. Matthew 10. 40; cf. 15. 24; Mark 9. 37; John 13. 20; 6. 44; 7. 16; cf. Isa. 6. 8; Jer. 26. 15; 28. 15.
6. Mark 6. 4; Luke 4. 24; 13. 33–4; John 4. 44.
7. 1 Sam. 8. 7; cf. Exod. 16. 8.

Similarly, Jesus in the Fourth Gospel cries out and says:

> He who rejects me and does not receive my sayings has a judge; the word that I have spoken will be his judge on the last day. For I have not spoken on my own authority; the Father who sent me has himself given me commandment what to say and what to speak.[1]

This is the authentic idiom of prophecy and in line with Micaiah's declaration: 'As the LORD lives, what the LORD says to me, that I will speak.'[2] Like the great prophets, Jesus was a man set under authority[3] and entrusted with authority,[4] known of God[5] and consecrated by him,[6] charged with an inescapable and heart-breaking mission. It is as difficult to find direct evidence of the personal consciousness of Jesus, as it is to penetrate the inner nature of the prophets' awareness. We know, however, that both Jesus and the prophets found temptation in the path of their vocation and knew the price of obedience. We need only recall the anguish of Jeremiah:

> For whenever I speak, I cry out,
>> I shout, 'Violence and destruction!'
> For the word of the LORD has become for me
>> a reproach and derision all day long.
> If I say, 'I will not mention him,
>> or speak any more in his name,'
> there is in my heart as it were a burning fire
>> shut up in my bones,
> and I am weary with holding it in,
>> and I cannot.[7]

With this in mind, we can better appreciate the agony of Jesus:

> I came to cast fire upon the earth; and would that it were already kindled! I have a baptism to be baptized with; and how I am constrained until it is accomplished! Do you think that I have come to give peace on earth? No, I tell you, but rather division.[8]

1. John 12. 48–9; cf. 5. 23; 15. 23; Luke 10. 16.
2. 1 Kings 22. 14; cf. Jer. 1. 7, 17, and pp. 37f.
3. John 4. 34; 5. 30; Amos 3. 8.
4. Matthew 28. 18; John 3. 35; 5. 27; Jer. 1. 10.
5. John 10. 15; Jer. 12. 3.　　　6. John 10. 36; Jer. 1. 5.
7. Jer. 20. 8–9.　　　8. Luke 12. 49–51.

The fundamental God-ward reference of Jesus' prophetic awareness has been more than a little obscured by doctrinal debate about the nature of his Person. His marked unwillingness to allow his followers to define the character of his mission is part of his unselfconsciousness, his wonderful self-effacement. Unless we see the sovereignty of God shining through our doctrines of the Person of Christ, they must be discarded as masks which conceal the single source of his lordship:

> I can do nothing on my own authority; as I *hear*, I judge; and my judgement is just, because I seek not my own will but the will of him who sent me.[1]

When we affirm, as we must, that Jesus was 'more than a prophet',[2] we are affirming the absolute completeness and, therefore, the uniqueness of his prophetic vocation. Without employing formal doctrinal language, we may emphasize the distinction between Jesus and (let us say) Jeremiah, by noticing how Jeremiah still clings to a residuum of self-will, which Jesus has extirpated in perfect devotion to the Father:

> O LORD, thou knowest;
>> remember me and visit me,
>> and take vengeance for me on
>>> my persecutors.
> In thy forbearance take me not away;
>> know that for thy sake I bear reproach.
> Thy words were found, and I ate them,
>> and thy words became to me a joy
>> and the delight of my heart;
> for I am called by thy name,
>> O LORD, God of hosts.[3]

The agony in Gethsemane leads to a very different conclusion:

> And he said to them, 'My soul is very sorrowful, even to death; remain here, and watch.' And going a little farther, he fell on the ground and prayed that, if it were possible, the hour might pass from him. And he said, 'Abba, Father, all things are possible to thee; remove this cup from me; yet not what I will, but what thou wilt.'[4]

1. John 5. 30.   2. Cf. Luke 7. 26.
3. Jer. 15. 15–16.   4. Mark 14. 34–6.

Whereas the prophets rebelled from time to time against the personal and moral obligations of their vocation, Jesus never rebelled. Like the prophets, he heard and proclaimed the Word of the Lord, but, unlike the prophets, he was in life always as good as his word. By his willing obedience, his infinite goodness, he made God's Word his own. That is why at the beginning of the Fourth Gospel, the evangelist can say simply that Jesus himself *was* the Word – the whole counsel and purpose of the eternal God embodied in human flesh.

In Jesus, the great prophets' awareness of God found fulfilment. The righteousness in terms of which they had spoken of the Kingdom of God became in the life and teaching of Jesus a present and final demand. His conviction that the Kingdom had come and was confronting men with a call to absolute righteousness is the assumption on which, for example, the whole Sermon on the Mount is founded:

You have heard that it was said, 'You shall love your neighbour and hate your enemy.' But *I say to you*, Love your enemies and pray for those who persecute you, so that you may be sons of your Father who is in heaven.[1]

Jesus spoke with authority and not as the scribes. This firm but quiet assumption of authority, for which (especially in the Fourth Gospel) the term 'kingship' is occasionally used,[2] is the evidence of Jesus' personal realization of the central theme of his teaching – the inauguration of the kingly Rule of God. What was of faith and the future for the prophets was for Jesus a present and overwhelming reality:

Blessed are the eyes which see what you see! For I tell you that many prophets and kings desired to see what you see, and did not see it, and to hear what you hear, and did not hear it.[3]

But if it is by the finger of God that I cast out demons, then the kingdom of God has come upon you.[4]

Jesus came into Galilee, preaching the gospel of God, and saying, 'The time is fulfilled, and the kingdom of God is at hand.'[5]

The whole of the New Testament is a commentary on the

1. Matthew 5. 43–5; cf. 5. 22, 28, 34, 39; Mark 1. 27.
2. Luke 19. 38; Matthew 21. 5; John 12. 15; cf. Zech. 9. 9; John 1. 49; 18. 37; 19. 15, 21–2; Revelation 17. 14; 19. 16.
3. Luke 10. 23–4.   4. Luke 11. 20.
5. Mark 1. 14–15; cf. Matthew 4. 17; 10. 7; Luke 10. 9; 17. 21.

proclamation that 'the time is fulfilled'. Fulfilment is that in which its essential newness consists. The first Christians were convinced that, in the life, death, and resurrection of Jesus, God had decisively accomplished that purpose which he disclosed in history when he called Israel to be his people.[1] When they looked forward to the Last Day in the imminent future,[2] they were not only recognizing the realities of a world in which only too obviously the Reign of God was not fully acknowledged, but also, by their conviction that the time was '*very short*',[3] they were affirming that in Christ the decisive event had already taken place and that 'the hour is coming *and now is*'.[4]

The New Testament is unintelligible until we have kept company with the prophets of the Old Testament, grasped their conception of God's purpose in Israel's calling and history, understood their conviction concerning Israel's judgement and restoration, and shared their vision of the new People of God to be established in that day when God reigned as King of the whole world. The New Testament proclaims that God-in-Christ has accomplished the purpose disclosed in Israel's prophetic history, achieved the end to which it was directed, and initiated the fulfilment to which the prophets looked forward in faith.

The prophecies are fulfilled and the Day of the Lord is *here*.[5] In his obedience to God, Christ had assumed the role of the Suffering Servant of the Lord[6] and given himself as a 'covenant to the people'.[7] Thus Jeremiah's faith in the inauguration of a New Covenant was actualized[8] – that New

1. See the records of the earliest apostolic preaching in Acts 13. 17–41; 2. 14–39; 3. 12–26; 10. 36–43; cf. 1 Corinthians 15. 1–7.

2. Acts 1. 11; 3. 19–21; 10. 42; 1 Thessalonians 4. 15–17; 1 Corinthians 15. 51–2; 16. 22; Romans 2. 16; 1 Peter 1. 5; 4. 7; 1 John 2. 18; Matthew 16. 28; Revelation 22. 6–7, 20.

3. 1 Corinthians 7. 29.   4. John 5. 25.

5. 1 Corinthians 15. 4 ('according to the scriptures'); Acts 2. 16; 3. 18, 24.

6. Mark 10. 45; cf. Isa. 53. 11–12 and pp. 87ff.

7. Isa. 42. 6; 49. 8; Zech. 9. 11; 1 Corinthians 11. 25; Luke 22. 20; Mark 14. 24; Matthew 26. 28.

8. Jer. 31. 31–4; cf. Hebrews 8. 8–13; II Corinthians 3. 6; 5. 17; Colossians 3. 9–10; see, further, p. 82.

Covenant by which the New Israel was established. For the writers of the New Testament, the New Israel of God is none other than the Church of Christ,[1] born of the Spirit, heir to prophetic history and a universal fellowship, in which God makes available all that he purposed for his people from the first. This is what St Luke is saying in his account of the birthday of the Christian Church on the first Whit Sunday:

> When the day of Pentecost had come, they were all together in one place. And suddenly a sound came from heaven like the rush of a mighty wind, and it filled all the house where they were sitting. And there appeared to them tongues as of fire, distributed and resting on each one of them. And they were all filled with the Holy Spirit and began to speak in other tongues, as the Spirit gave them utterance.
>
> Now there were dwelling in Jerusalem Jews, devout men from every nation under heaven. And at this sound the multitude came together, and they were bewildered, because each one heard them speaking in his own language. ... And all were amazed and perplexed, saying to one another, 'What does this mean?' But others mocking said, 'They are filled with new wine.'
>
> But Peter, standing with the eleven, lifted up his voice and addressed them, 'Men of Judea and all who dwell in Jerusalem, let this be known to you, and give ear to my words. For these men are not drunk, as you suppose, since it is only the third hour of the day; but *this is what was spoken by the prophet Joel*:
>
> "And *in the last days* it shall be, God declares,
>   that I will pour out my Spirit upon all flesh,
>   and your sons and your daughters shall prophesy,
>   and your young men shall see visions,
>   and your old men shall dream dreams;
>   yea, and on my menservants and my maidservants *in those days*
>   I will pour out my Spirit; and they shall prophesy. ..."

Men of Israel, hear these words: Jesus of Nazareth, a man attested to you by God with mighty works and wonders and signs which God did through him in your midst, as you yourselves know – this Jesus, delivered up according to the definite plan and foreknowledge of God, you crucified and killed by the hands of lawless men. ... This Jesus God raised up, and of that we all are witnesses. Being therefore exalted at the right hand of God, and having received from the

1. Galatians 3. 29; 6. 16; Romans 4. 13–15; 11. 5; 1 Peter 2. 9–10; cf. Luke 22. 28–30; Acts 3. 25–6; Revelation 5. 10.

Father the promise of the Holy Spirit, he has poured out this which you see and hear. ...'

Now when they heard this they were cut to the heart, and said to Peter and the rest of the apostles, 'Brethren, what shall we do?' And Peter said to them, 'Repent, and be baptized every one of you in the name of Jesus Christ for the forgiveness of your sins; and you shall receive the gift of the Holy Spirit. ... ' So those who received his word were baptized, and there were added that day about three thousand souls. And they devoted themselves to the apostles' teaching and fellowship, to the breaking of bread and the prayers.[1]

There was a Jewish tradition that at Sinai, when Israel entered into the first covenant, 'every people received the law in their own language.' So here, at the inauguration of the new Israel, people from every nation under heaven are said to have heard in their own language the 'mighty works of God'. St Luke intends his readers to understand that the universal fellowship of the Church is the climax of that redemptive work in history which God began with his calling of Israel. The People of God is his answer to the sin of mankind.[2] There is also a second line of thought which should be recognized. In the parable of the Tower of Babel in Genesis, man's sin is symbolized by the confusion of languages.[3] That confusion is now overcome by the gift of the prophetic spirit. The unity of the Christian fellowship is Babel reversed.

When the Church is true to its vocation as the *prophetic* community in which the purpose of God is discerned, proclaimed, and actively pursued, the world will say of it, as the old writer represented God as saying of the men of Babel: 'Behold, they are one people, and they have all one language; and this is only the beginning of what they will do; and nothing that they propose to do will now be impossible for them.'[4]

1. Acts 2. 1–42 (abbreviated); see Joel 2. 28–32 and p. 160.
2. See pp. 59f.   3. Gen. 11. 1–9.
4. Gen. 11. 6; cf. Mark 10. 27; Zech. 4. 6; 8. 6.

APPENDIX I

THE POLITICAL AND PROPHETIC
HISTORY OF ISRAEL

POLITICAL

The semi-nomadic life of the Patriarchs in the Fertile Crescent (2000–1700).

The Hebrews in Egypt (from about 1400).

The Exodus from Egypt and the Covenant at the Mount of God (about ? 1280).

The Conquest of Palestine (about 1240–1200).

The period of the Judges (about 1200–1020).

The founding of the Monarchy:
Saul (1020–1000),
David (1000–965),
Solomon (965–926), who built the Temple.
In 926 the kingdom split into:
The kingdom of Israel (926–721).
The kingdom of Judah (926–586).

PROPHETIC

§ 1. *Israel's Call and Covenant*

'Brethren, sons of the family of Abraham, and those among you that fear God, to us has been sent the message of this salvation'
(Acts 13. 26).

ABRAHAM (about 1900)

'The God of this people Israel chose our fathers and made the people great during their stay in the land of Egypt, and with uplifted arm he led them out of it'
(Acts 13. 17).

MOSES (about 1280)

'And for about forty years he bore with them in the wilderness'
(Acts 13. 18).

§ 2. *God's Gift of the Land*

'And when he had destroyed seven nations in the land of Canaan, he gave them their land as an inheritance...and after that he gave them judges until Samuel the prophet' (Acts 13. 19–20).

DAVID (about 1000–965)

'Then they asked for a king; and God gave them Saul the son of Kish...and when he had removed him, he raised up David to be their king' (Acts 13. 21–2).

§ 3. *Prophetic Interpreters of the Covenant*

'Surely the Lord GOD does nothing, without revealing his secret to his servants the prophets'

(Amos 3. 7).

ELIJAH (about 850)

Ahab, king of Israel (871–852); Jezebel, his wife, was a menace to the religion of Israel.

'I have been very jealous for the LORD, the God of hosts; for the people of Israel have forsaken thy covenant, thrown down thy altars, and slain thy prophets with the sword' (1 Kings 19. 10).

AMOS (about 750)

Great material prosperity in Israel during the reign of Jeroboam II (787–747).
The beginning of the Assyrian supremacy (745–625).

'You only have I known
of all the families of the earth;
therefore I will punish you
for all your iniquities'

(Amos 3. 2).

HOSEA (about 745)

A period of great instability in the Israelite monarchy.

'How can I give you up, O Ephraim!' (Hosea 11. 8).

ISAIAH (about 742–700)

Ahaz, king of Judah (742–725).
Syro-Ephraimitic War (734).

'Take heed, be quiet, do not fear, and do not let your heart be faint'

(Isa. 7. 4).

MICAH (about 725)

Hezekiah, king of Judah (725–697).
The fall of Samaria to Assyria and *the end of the kingdom of Israel* (721).
The Assyrian siege of Jerusalem (701).

'Therefore because of you
Zion shall be plowed as a field;
Jerusalem shall become a heap of
ruins,
and the mountain of the house a
wooded height'

(Mic. 3. 12).

Increase of paganism in Judah during the reign of Manasseh (696–642), followed by the Reform of Josiah (640–609).

Zephaniah may have prophesied about 626.

The fall of Nineveh, the Assyrian capital, in 612 is celebrated in Nahum.

The beginning of the Babylonian supremacy (612–538).

Habakkuk may have prophesied about 600.

The first Babylonian invasion and deportation (597).

The second Babylonian invasion (588).

The Fall of Jerusalem and beginning of the Exile (586).

The victorious advance of Cyrus from about 550.

The Fall of Babylon (539).

§ 4. *Prophets of Judgement and Renewal*

'The LORD sent me to prophesy against this house and this city all the words you have heard'

(Jer. 26. 12).

JEREMIAH (about 626–586)

'Thus says the LORD of hosts, the God of Israel, to all the exiles whom I have sent into exile from Jerusalem to Babylon: Build houses and live in them; plant gardens and eat their produce'   (Jer. 29. 4–5).

EZEKIEL (?593–572)

'You shall dwell in the land which I gave to your fathers; and you shall be my people, and I will be your God'   (Ezek. 36. 28).

§ 5. *Prophets of the Coming Kingdom*

'Incline your ear, and come to me;
        hear, that your soul may live;
and I will make with you an ever-
                lasting covenant,
        my steadfast, sure love for David'
                (Isa. 55. 3).

SECOND ISAIAH (about 540)

'Get you up to a high mountain,
        O herald of good tidings to Zion;
lift up your voice with strength,
        O herald of good tidings to Jer-
                usalem,
        lift it up, fear not;
say to the cities of Judah,
        "Behold your God!"'
                (Isa. 40. 9).

After 538, the Jews began to return to Jerusalem and Zerubbabel was appointed governor.

The accession of Darius I in 522 was followed by revolutions throughout the Persian Empire.

The second Temple was completed in 516.

Nehemiah, governor of Judah (444), rebuilt the walls of Jerusalem.

The imperial rulers of the Jews:
The Persians (538–331).
The Greeks (331–63).
The Romans (from 63).

Herod the Great, by a decision of the Roman Senate, king of the Jews (40–4 B.C.).

Anno Domini

HAGGAI (520)

'Speak to Zerubbabel, governor of Judah, saying, I am about to shake the heavens and the earth, and to overthrow the throne of kingdoms' (Hag. 2. 21–2).

ZECHARIAH (520–518)

'Thus says the LORD: I will return to Zion, and will dwell in the midst of Jerusalem'
(Zech. 8. 3).

MANY NAMELESS PROPHETS (including the authors of Isaiah 56–66, Malachi, Jonah) AND JOEL

'And the LORD will become king over all the earth; on that day the LORD will be one and his name one'
(Zech. 14. 9).

§ 6. *The Coming of the Kingdom*

'Before his coming John had preached a baptism of repentance to all the people of Israel'
(Acts 13. 24).

JOHN THE BAPTIST

'After me one is coming, the sandals of whose feet I am not worthy to untie' (Acts 13. 25).

JESUS

'The time is fulfilled, and the kingdom of God is at hand'
(Mark 1. 15).

Judgement

'For those who live in Jerusalem and their rulers, because they did not recognize him nor understand the utterances of the prophets which are read every sabbath, fulfilled these by condemning him.

Pontius Pilate, procurator of Judea (A.D. 26–36).

Though they could charge him with nothing deserving death, yet they asked Pilate to have him killed' (Acts 13. 27–8).

Renewal

'But God raised him from the dead; and for many days he appeared to those who came up with him from Galilee to Jerusalem, who are now his witnesses to the people. And we bring you the good news that what God promised to the fathers, this he has fulfilled to us their children by raising Jesus'

(Acts 13. 30–3).

§ 7. *The New Israel*

The first Council of the Church at Jerusalem about A.D. 49 recognized the admission of Gentiles.

'But you are a chosen race, a royal priesthood, a holy nation, God's own people, that you may declare the wonderful deeds of him who called you out of darkness into his marvellous light. Once you were no people but now you are God's people; once you had not received mercy but now you have received mercy' (1 Peter 2. 9–10).

A GUIDE TO FURTHER READING

As the purpose of this small book is to stimulate interest in the prophetic faith of the People of God, the difficult task of selecting books for further reading is unavoidable. The task is difficult, because the overwhelming bulk of the books written about the Old Testament have a bearing on our subject; but simply to list a great number of them would achieve no useful purpose. What follows, therefore, is selective.

For the reader who is quite new to Bible study, it may be useful to mention three or four simple books which place the Old Testament prophets in the context of the Bible as a whole. Two stand out from the rest:

The Bible To-day, C. H. Dodd, Cambridge University Press (1946).
The Rediscovery of the Bible, W. Neil, Hodder and Stoughton (1954).

Once the overall shape of the Bible has been grasped, more detailed information may be found in *The Authority of the Bible*, C. H. Dodd, Nisbet (1928), and *An Introduction to the Bible*, Stanley Cook, Pelican (1945). Among the scores of books which give a general conspectus of the Old Testament (as distinct from the whole Bible), *A Foreword to the Old Testament*, H. St J. Hart, Black (1951), and *The Religious Ideas of the Old Testament*, H. W. Robinson, Duckworth (1913), are both masterly and easy to read.

As the study of Hebrew prophecy inevitably raises a number of disputed points of interpretation, it is most desirable that more than one writer's opinion should be consulted. To supplement (and, where necessary, to correct) the presentation in the preceding chapters, one (especially the first) of the following general books on the prophets is recommended for further reading:

The Relevance of the Prophets, R. B. Y. Scott, Macmillan (1944).
The Prophets and their Times, J. M. P. Smith, revised by W. A. Irwin, Chicago University Press (1941).
The Prophets of Israel, Curt Kuhl, Oliver and Boyd (1960).

Martin Buber's *The Prophetic Faith* (trans. C. Witton-Davies, Macmillan (1949)) is too difficult for the beginner, but a student who is prepared to concentrate will find his efforts fully rewarded.

If a copy of *The Prophets of Israel* by that great pioneer, W. Robertson Smith, and first published in 1882, is ever found on a second-hand bookstall, it should be bought immediately. The depth of its insight far outweighs the fact that its critical scholarship is not up-to-date.

Those who can most easily grasp the significance of a tradition by studying representative personalities will find much instruction and enjoyment in Fleming James' *Personalities of the Old Testament*, Scribner's (1939), or in W. A. L. Elmslie's learned (but lively) *How Came Our Faith*, Cambridge University Press (1947). Less popular in presentation, but equally straightforward in content, is *Kings and Prophets of Israel*, A. C. Welch, ed. N. W. Porteous, Lutterworth (1952).

There are many excellent studies of individual prophets, among which John Skinner's big book on Jeremiah, *Prophecy and Religion*, Cambridge University Press (1922), is probably still supreme. This might with advantage (but with a fair degree of intellectual effort) be followed by a reading of *Jeremiah: His Time and His Work*, A. C. Welch, Blackwell (1951). The same prophet shares H. W. Robinson's *The Cross in the Old Testament*, S.C.M. Press (1955), with Second Isaiah and Job. Few would dispute the opinion that everything written by H. Wheeler Robinson is eminently readable and eminently worth reading and he has left us his mature (but brief) reflections on Hosea and Ezekiel in *Two Hebrew Prophets*, Lutterworth (1948).

When we come to studying the actual text of the prophetic books with commentaries, there is something for everybody. The most concise treatment will be found in the one-volume commentaries of the Bible, of which two are recent and up-to-date publications:

Concise Bible Commentary, W. K. Lowther Clarke, S.P.C.K. (1952).
The Teachers' Commentary, ed. G. Henton Davies and A. Richardson, S.C.M. Press (1955).

Those who have access to Peake's *Commentary* (of which an entirely new edition is expected from Nelson in 1961) or to *The Abingdon Commentary*, Abingdon Press (1929), will find a great deal of introductory material in them which is very valuable. For most readers, however, the annotated selections of *The Clarendon Bible*, Oxford University Press, will prove most generally useful. The following four volumes contain selections from the prophetic books:

Vol. II: *From Moses to Elisha*, L. Elliott-Binns (1929).
Vol. III: *The Decline and Fall of the Hebrew Kingdoms*, T. H. Robinson (1926).

Appendix II

Vol. IV: *Israel after the Exile*, W. F. Lofthouse (1928).
Vol. V: *Judaism in the Greek Period*, G. H. Box (1932).

In *The Torch Commentaries*, S.C.M. Press, volumes on the prophets include C. R. North, *Isaiah 40–55*, J. Marsh, *Amos and Micah*, G. A. F. Knight, *Ruth and Jonah* and *Hosea*, and H. Cunliffe-Jones, *Jeremiah*. For readers who have passed the first stages of Old Testament study, *The Interpreter's Bible*, Abingdon and Nelson, will almost certainly open up a new world. The Authorized and Revised Standard Versions of the text are printed in parallel columns at the top of each page; an admirably concise exegesis occupies the centre of the page; and at the bottom of the page there is a wide-ranging exposition of the religious significance of the text. The fifth volume (1956) includes commentaries on Isaiah 1–39, Isaiah 40–66, and Jeremiah, of which the second is superlatively good. The sixth volume (1956) gives commentaries on the Twelve Minor Prophets and a most valuable commentary on the enigmatic book of Ezekiel. Although these handsome volumes are splendid value for money and almost essential for the serious student, they *are* expensive. It is worth mentioning, therefore, that volumes of the *Century Bible*, published by Jack, may often be picked up second-hand and, generally speaking, are well worth buying.

Information about the historical background, dating, and literary problems of the prophetic books may be found in immense (and rather overwhelming) detail in *Introduction to the Old Testament*, R. H. Pfeiffer, Black (1952), and in lucid, summary form in *A Critical Introduction to the Old Testament*, G. W. Anderson, Duckworth (1959).

The subject of our Chapter 2, 'The Vocation of the Prophets', may be followed up in H. Knight's interesting study, *The Hebrew Prophetic Consciousness*, Lutterworth (1947), but the serious student will not be content until he has investigated the following:

The Servant of the Lord, H. H. Rowley, Lutterworth (1952), Chapter 3.
Inspiration and Revelation in the Old Testament, H. W. Robinson, Oxford University Press (1946).
Studies in Old Testament Prophecy, ed. H. H. Rowley, Clark (1950).
Record and Relevation, ed. H. W. Robinson, Oxford University Press (1938), for the essay on 'Prophecy' by N. W. Porteous.
The Old Testament and Modern Study, ed. H. H. Rowley, Oxford University Press (1951), for the essay on 'The Prophetic Literature' by O. Eissfeldt.

The subject of Chapter 3, 'The Vocation of the People', is discussed in *The Biblical Doctrine of Election*, H. H. Rowley, Lutterworth (1950), and more simply by the same writer in *The Missionary Message of the Old Testament*, Carey Press (1945). The theme of Israel's Election is emphasized in the writings of G. E. Wright, who contributes the section on 'The Faith of Israel' in the first volume of *The Interpreter's Bible*, Abingdon and Nelson (1952). He has also published two relevant monographs – *The Old Testament Against its Environment* (1950) and *God Who Acts* (1952) in the S.C.M. Press's 'Studies in Biblical Theology'. On the same subject, *The Old Testament Interpretation of History*, C. R. North, Epworth Press (1946), will be found easy to read and most illuminating.

The general religious and historical background of the prophets is well documented. The most useful brief account of the history (clearly related to the ministries of the prophets) is *The History of Israel*, H. W. Robinson, Duckworth (1938). Among the larger histories, two are quite outstanding – M. Noth, *The History of Israel*, Black (revised edition, 1960) and John Bright, *A History of Israel*, S.C.M. Press (1960). The latter is particularly valuable for the clarity of its presentation. The religious background is authoritatively presented in *Biblical Archaeology*, G. E. Wright, Duckworth (1957), and sketched in popular form in the present writer's *Everyday Life in Old Testament Times*, Batsford (1956). The relationship between prophet and priest is much debated and may be studied in *Prophet and Priest in Old Israel*, A. C. Welch, Blackwell (1953), and A. R. Johnson's more advanced monograph, *The Cultic Prophet in Ancient Israel*, University of Wales Press (1944). The prophets' attitude to sacrifice is interpreted in a way which the present writer cannot accept in *The Unity of the Bible*, H. H. Rowley, Carey Kingsgate Press (1953), Chapter 2.

On the subject of our last chapter, 'Faith and Fulfilment', G. W. Anderson's translation of *He That Cometh*, S. Mowinckel, Blackwell (1956), is clearly the key-book for the advanced student. It cannot, however, be called easy reading, and a more simple presentation may be found in *The Christian Significance of the Old Testament*, A. J. B. Higgins, Independent Press (1949). For the early Christians' use of the Old Testament prophets, *According to the Scriptures*, C. H. Dodd, Nisbet (1952), is of fundamental importance. Readers who cannot manage a discussion involving New Testament Greek are advised to consult the same writer's pamphlet, *The Old Testament in the New*, Athlone Press (1952).

Finally, a recent work by John Bright, *The Kingdom of God in Bible and Church*, Lutterworth (1955), deserves special notice. As the title suggests, it develops one of the themes which the preceding chapters have attempted to elucidate. The solid appearance of the book belies the easy and forceful style in which it is written. As an exposition of the theology of the Bible as a whole, it is strongly recommended.

INDEX OF SUBJECTS

Index of Subjects

Devotion, 65
Divination, 38, 40 f., 72, 125
Dogmatists, 90 f.
Dreams, 42

Ecclesiastes, 137
Ecclesiasticus, 33, 110
Ecstasy, 41 f., 51
Edom, 20, 117
Egypt, 26, 56 f., 76, 153 f., 172; *see also* Exodus
Election of Israel, 21, 69 f., 84–7, 156 f., Chap. 3, *passim*
Elijah, 34 f., 43 ff., 105 f., 165, 173
Elisha, 39, 43
Enthronement, 131
Esau, 59
Ethics, Chap. 4, *passim*
Exile, the, 19, 21, 25, 55, 81 f., 83–89, 99, 138–49, 174
Exodus, the, 56 ff., 60 f., 63, 66 ff., 70, 97, 118, 157 f.
Exodus, the Second, 67, 84, 157
Ezekiel, 28 f., 32, 53, 99, 141 f., 150 f., 160, 174
Ezra, 84

Faith, 75–9
False prophets, 34, 36–40, 125
Family life, 50, 63, 103, 120 f., 134
Fees for prophecy, 38 f.
Fertile Crescent, 73 f.
Fertility rites, 71 f.
Foreknowledge, 125–30
Forgiveness, 72 f.
Friendship, 45 f., 63 f.
Fulfilment in Christ, 14–17, 28, Chap. 5, *passim* ; *see also* Jesus Christ
Future life, 134–7

Genesis, 59 f., 67 f.
Gentiles, 21, 59 f., 89, 117 f., 143, 151–7, 176
Geography, 73 f.

Gethsemane, 167
Glory of God, 52, 122, 142
Gog of Magog, 152
Gomer, 72
Gomorrah, 73
Good Time Coming, 150–63
Grace of God, 142
Greeks, influence of, 12, 135
Guilds, prophetic, 35 f., 37 f., 39 f., 43
Guilt and punishment, 97 ff.

Habakkuk, 22, 174
Haggai, 23, 84, 148 f., 175
Hebrews, Epistle to, 13, 82
Herod the Great, 175
ḥeṣedh, 64 f.
Hezekiah, 173
High-places, 71 f., 109–14
History and prophecy, 66 ff., 77 ff., 83 f., 86 f., 100 f., 117 f., 125–30, 172–5; *see also* Exodus, Exile
Holiness, 122 f., 141 f., 150
Horeb, 44
Hosea, 18, 49, 65, 71 ff., 173
Humanists, 90 f.

Idiom, Hebrew, 53 f., 101–4
Idols, 72, 83, 85, 93, 129
Immanuel oracle, 76
Immortality, 134–7
Incarnation, the, 14, 100, 168; *see also* Jesus Christ
Individual and community, 95–100, 137
Innocent suffering, 97 ff.
Interpretation, biblical, 11–17, 162 f.
Isaac, 59, 68
Isaiah, 25 f., 52 ff., 56, 73–9, 85, 122, 127, 144 ff., 158, 160 ff., 173
Israel, kingdom of, 55, 75, 172 f.
Israel, the New, 16, 170 ff., 176

Jacob, 59, 68
Jehoiachin, 148

Index of Subjects

*Some other books
on religion are described
on the following pages*

INTRODUCING CHRISTIANITY

E. H. Pyle and S. G. Williamson

WAI I

Here is a book about Christianity which is different, because it strips away some of the conventional trappings of the faith as it is practised in the world today. Believers and non-believers will read it with equal interest, as an objective description of the Western faith as it might appear, say, to an African. The authors, although they are committed Christians, try to do no more than 'introduce' a religion which in essence claims to be unique. They provide a background for the story of Jesus by explaining the beliefs of the Jews he addressed; they speak factually of Jesus and of the people who knew him, and go on to describe the work of St Paul and the Church's expansion.

Although the book makes it clear that Christianity is unlike any other faith, it emphasises that race, colour, class, caste, sex, or age can never exclude a human being from the fellowship of the Church.

This book is one of the Penguin African Series, especially designed to provide background information and front-rank comment concerning this increasingly important continent.

GOD IN ACTION

F. A. Cockin

A513

God in Action is about the third person of the Trinity – the Holy Spirit. Bishop Cockin is convinced that a great deal of the Church's weakness and lack of effective leadership in contemporary society springs from neglect of the workings of the Spirit.

The urgent tasks of the Church, such as the rehabilitation of the Christian way of life in an unbelieving world; the bringing of Christianity to industrial and family life; and the achievement of a break-out from the stalemate of disunity – all these he relates to the fact of the Spirit as he appears in the New Testament and in Christian experience.

The author maintains that the thought, work, and worship of the Church must be invigorated and largely transformed by the recovery of the sense of God's Spirit speaking through the events of our own lives – and that this indeed is the Biblical outlook.